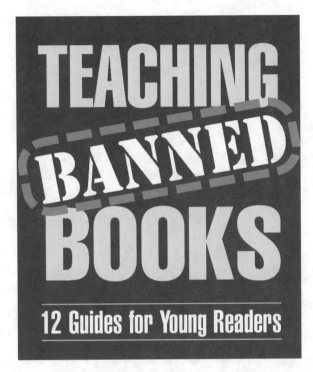

PAT R. SCALES

AMERICAN LIBRARY ASSOCIATION

Chicago and London

2001

Cover by Tessing Design

Text design by Dianne M. Rooney

Composition by ALA Editions using QuarkXpress 4.1 for the PC

Printed on 50-pound white offset, a pH-neutral stock, and bound in 10-point cover stock by Batson Printing

The paper used in this publication meets the minimum requirements of American National Standard for Information Sciences—Permanence of Paper for Printed Library Materials, ANSI Z39.48-1992. ∞

Library of Congress Cataloging-in-Publication Data

Scales, Pat.
    Teaching banned books : 12 guides for young readers / Pat R. Scales.
        p. cm.
    Includes bibliographical references and index.
    ISBN 0-8389-0807-1 (alk. paper)
    1. Challenged books—United States. 2. Children's literature, American—Study and teaching (Middle school)—United States. 3. Freedom of speech—Study and teaching (Middle school)—United States. 4. Middle school libraries—Activity programs—United States 5. Middle school students—Books and reading—United States. I. Title.
    Z1019 .S33 2001
    098'.1'071—dc21   2001022340

Printed in the United States of America

05 04 03 02 01   5 4 3 2 1

For

Indiana P. Thomas

my loyal and dedicated assistant

for nineteen years

and

the woman who taught me courage

and the true meaning of freedom—

from free speech to civil rights

CONTENTS

PART ONE
The First Amendment, Censorship, and Intellectual Freedom

PART TWO
The Bully and the Outcasts

PART THREE
Racism, Bigotry, and Civil Rights

PART FOUR
Reality, Secrets, and the Imagination

PART FIVE
Other Worlds, Other Cultures, and Other Times

FOREWORD

If we could clone educators, I'd clone Pat Scales and send her to guide, support, and encourage every new school librarian and teacher. But until that's a possibility, I'll just have to spread the word any way I can. For those of you who aren't familiar with her work, I'll begin in the mid-1970s when Pat's students at Greenville Middle School in Greenville, South Carolina, did a telephone interview with me. Their questions were thoughtful, sometimes difficult, and often laced with humor. I got the feeling they listened to my answers as carefully as they had prepared their questions. So I was pleased when Pat and I finally met in person, a year or so later at Pat's first ALA conference. My editor, Dick Jackson, invited Pat to join his table at the Newbery-Caldecott dinner. I'd never been to a Newbery-Caldecott celebration, either. I still remember what I wore because I had recently moved to New Mexico and I came decked out in a long, gauzy number, with silver and turquoise around my neck. More importantly, I remember Mildred Taylor's acceptance speech for *Roll of Thunder, Hear My Cry*.

It wasn't easy to talk at that dinner but when I heard about Communicate through Literature, the program Pat had started at Greenville Middle School, I was fascinated. Here was a young school librarian inviting the parents of her students into her library once a month, without the kids, to talk about contemporary young adult books. Her goals were to help them get comfortable with the books their children might be reading, and to encourage them to use literature to spark open and honest conversations with their kids. In doing so, Pat helped these parents remember their own adolescent years, bringing back all those feelings they had managed to forget, and eased their fears and concerns about having their kids read books dealing with real life. Before long, in Greenville, parents and kids were sharing books. Pat was right—the characters in these novels made it easier to talk about subjects and feelings that were on the kids' minds, though until now they had never brought them up at home.

In 1981, when I started The Kids Fund, a small foundation whose goal it was to help bring parents and kids together (because by then I was receiving volumes of mail from kids who wished they could talk openly and honestly with their parents), Pat Scales and Communicate through Literature were our first grant recipient. The stipend was small but somehow the *Today* show got word of it and asked if they could do a story on Pat's program. When Pat agreed, they sent a film crew to Greenville to interview some of her students and their parents.

Pat and I appeared on the show together, live from New York, to talk about her work. What I remember best about our segment (aside from how nervous we were and that Pat was wearing blue) was that after showing clips of parents and kids at home talking about books, Bryant Gumbel came at us as if approaching the enemy. He led off his attack with, "Yeeah. . . but will it play in Peoria?" His manner and question left me speechless but Pat's priceless answer, a long, perplexed "Huh . . . ?" said it all.

Undaunted by her experience on the *Today* show, Pat went back to Greenville and continued to do what she does best—teach and communicate. She worked with her students, their parents, and other librarians and teachers. In 1983, she was honored by the American Association of School Librarians with the AASL/SIRS Intellectual Freedom Award for her Communicate through Literature program.

At a time when fear was starting to creep into both the school library and the classroom, when some school principals were beginning to worry about anything that could be taken as controversial, and you never knew when some zealot might come into your library, waving a book and demanding its removal, Pat never had an issue with censorship. Maybe because parents and students alike trusted and respected her, just as she trusted and respected them. Maybe because she could always explain, in a clear and sensible way, why the books in her program were important to her students. And maybe she was just lucky (not all teachers and librarians survived that era). Luck or not, Pat would fight to her last breath to protect the rights of her students. She's helped me and countless others in defending the rights of all young people to be intellectually free. Most recently she's been telling me, with her usual enthusiasm, about teaching the First Amendment to eighth graders and high school students. And I've been yapping, in my usual way, about sharing her methods with other librarians and teachers. So I welcome this book with my own enthusiasm and high hopes. And say, once again, thanks, Pat. Bravo!

JUDY BLUME

PREFACE

I think I have always been a proponent of the freedom to read; I just didn't know how to articulate it until I was an adult and established in my career. I don't feel that my reading was ever censored at home as a child. My dad was a great reader, and from my early adolescence, I read most of what he read. There was no young adult literature in those days so I read John Steinbeck and Erskine Caldwell. Did these books affect me? Yes, for all the right reasons. They made me sensitive to society and the ways others live. I learned about other cultures by reading books like Pearl Buck's *The Good Earth*. I learned about our past by reading novels like *Gone with the Wind* and *Huckleberry Finn*. I knew then that the friendship between Huck Finn and Jim was special. I was able to understand what Huck Finn knew all along—friendship transcends race. I remember reading Arthur Miller's play *The Crucible* and thinking that nowhere in my American history book was there a discussion of the Salem witch trials. That was the crowning moment when I realized that textbooks and teachers had control over ideas and learning in the classroom. But, I was lucky. I had a dad who believed that you couldn't form your own ideas until you had read and thought about the ideas of others. You couldn't know about our history until you had read all our history, regardless of how ugly some of it may be.

I don't remember ever hearing the word *censorship.* But, as I look back, I realize that there was plenty of censorship by omission going on in schools. When I heard discussion in my college children's literature class about whether the monsters in Maurice Sendak's *Where the Wild Things Are* might scare children, I knew that the people who worried about that didn't know children. I listened to discussions about Garth Williams's *The Rabbit's Wedding* and wondered how we could possibly teach children to celebrate love and friendship in all forms if we didn't allow them to experience it through books.

By the time I became a librarian, I had completely dedicated myself to the ideas and ideals of intellectual freedom. About that time, Judy Blume came into the lives of young adolescent readers. All over the nation, her books were being challenged. But, my students were reading her because I was reading her. I was able to lead them to her books because I knew her books. I was able to talk about her books because I understood her books. During this time, I began to realize that having open discussions about books with children and teenagers is the best way to encourage freedom of thought. You teach by example. And I wanted to be an example of free expression. It was also about this time that I began a parent literature program at the middle school where I served as librarian. The idea was to have parents read the same books that their children were reading and to come together once a month to discuss these books. These parents understood that *Blubber* by Judy Blume is a harsh reality of the life of many fifth and sixth graders. But what they also learned was how to discuss this with their children. They began calling me and asking me for books about teenage sexuality, about death, and about dealing with bullies. And, we never had a censorship case.

The program for parents paved the way for teachers in this school to branch out and teach novels that have been censored and challenged throughout the nation. These books, like Brock Cole's *The Goats*, Robert Lipsyte's *One Fat Summer*, Jean Craighead George's *Julie of the Wolves*, Katherine Paterson's *Bridge to Terabithia*, Mildred Taylor's *Roll of Thunder, Hear My Cry*, and James and Christopher Collier's *My Brother Sam Is Dead*, are considered classics in the world of children's and young adult literature. But, censors don't care. All these books have recent challenges recorded by the American Library Association's Office for Intellectual Freedom. The teachers and I team-taught these novels, and we looked for other powerful novels like Suzanne Newton's *I Will Call It Georgie's Blues* that could make a lasting impact on young readers. It didn't matter to us that Neal Sloan, the main character of the novel, uses profanity to get his mother's attention. It didn't matter that some people might take offense at the way the Reverend Sloan is presented. It didn't matter, because we knew that we could have an open discussion with the students about these issues, and that through that discussion, they would better understand the conflict of the novel and the emotions of the character. I read *The Giver* by Lois Lowry and *The Watsons Go to Birmingham–1963* by Christopher Paul Curtis aloud to a group of 75 middle school students who gathered each morning to listen. It was amazing to watch the spontaneous discussion that erupted in the room at the end of each novel. These students had learned how to think, and how to express themselves.

These experiences led me to write this book. I really believe that students want to know about their rights. I believe that they have opinions and want to voice them. When adults try to shield students from the "darker side of life" or from ideas that may be controversial, such adults are creating a generation of skeptics and cynics who don't really know the meaning of free speech.

This book includes strategies for teaching 10 books for middle school readers that have been challenged or censored in this nation. Although numerous titles could have been included, I have chosen these 10 because most of them appear on the American Library Association's list of the *100 Most Frequently Challenged Books of 1990–1999*, and because I have had personal experience in teaching these novels. Though *The Watsons Go to Birmingham–1963*, *Roll of Thunder, Hear My Cry*, and *I Will Call It Georgie's Blues* are not on the list, I have personal knowledge of challenges to these novels. In addition to these 10 strategies, I have included a strategy for teaching the First Amendment to students. Students have an innate interest in their freedom of speech, but most know little about the subject. This strategy will perhaps encourage librarians, language arts teachers, and social studies teachers to make the First Amendment a vital part of the curriculum. Finally, I have included a strategy for teaching *Places I Never Meant to Be*, edited by Judy Blume, an anthology of 12 short stories by writers who have been censored. At the end of each story, its author discusses how censorship has affected his or her career as a writer. This book is a natural follow-up to teaching the First Amendment.

Each strategy includes a summary of the novel, a pre-reading activity, discussion questions that encourage critical thinking, and activities to broaden students' knowledge of topics in the novel. An annotated bibliography of related fiction and nonfiction accompanies each strategy. Six of these strategies were originally published in the "Book Strategies" column in *Book Links* magazine. The others were developed specifically for this book. The strategy for teaching *The Giver* was written by Julie Corsaro and appeared in *Book Links* magazine. The bibliographies have been updated, and some discussion questions specifically related to the challenges brought against the novel have been added to the previously published strategies.

It is my sincere belief that every time we listen to a student's opinion, we practice the principles of intellectual freedom. This isn't a responsibility for which many of us were prepared by teacher training or in library school. It is a learned responsibility, and it is ours.

ACKNOWLEDGMENTS

I wish to acknowledge:

Barbara Elleman, the founding editor of *Book Links* magazine, who asked me in 1990 over coffee in Indianapolis to be a part of this wonderful new magazine that she was starting.

Judy O'Malley, Barbara's successor, who listened and thought it was a great idea when I wanted to feature challenged books in the September issues of *Book Links*.

Jane Wassynger, Alonda Rollison, Sarah Smeal, Betty Jenkins, and the countless other teachers who asked me into their literature classrooms and shared their students with me through many novel studies, and for their own commitment to intellectual freedom.

The students of Greenville Middle School from 1972 to 1998 for allowing me into their lives so that we could learn and grow together—through books.

It can hardly be argued that either students or teachers shed their constitutional rights to freedom of speech or expression at the schoolhouse gate.

–Justice Abe Fortas,
*Tinker v. Des Moines
School District,* 1969

STRATEGY 1

Studying the First Amendment

Too many schools, too many teachers, too many communities are fearful of the one thing that education is supposed to achieve: the capacity to think.

—Peter Schrag

This is America! Yet, according to statistics gathered by the ALA Office for Intellectual Freedom and the National Coalition against Censorship, book challenges are at an epidemic level in school and public libraries across the United States. What is amiss in this "land of the free"? Is this "censorship war" about fear? Control? Power? Is it a fight between the "schooled" and the "unschooled"? The "sighted" and the "blind"? The "thinkers" and the "nonthinkers"? How does this battle affect the education of our children? What kind of messages are we sending to them regarding their constitutional rights?

When I was in library school, there was a course called Censorship. This course surveyed such books as *Portnoy's Complaint, Of Mice and Men,* and *The Catcher in the Rye.* This was in the days before Judy Blume, Robert Cormier, Stephen King, R. L. Stein, Nancy Garden, Katherine Paterson, J. K. Rowling, and Alvin Schwartz. It was in the days when public libraries had more challenges than school libraries. It was five years before Steven

Adapted from an article first published in *Book Links,* September 1995.

1

Pico and his fellow high school students took the Island Trees (New York) school board to court for removing books from the school library. Most library school students took this censorship course for personal enjoyment; they never realized that fighting censorship could become a very real part of their job. Today, the battle is raging, and public librarians and school library media specialists are stumbling in their fight to win the war. The enemy is organized groups of people, from the right and the left, who are determined to gain power over what students read, learn, and view. In some cities, library boards are under pressure to place ratings on books and to install Internet filters. In other places, students' names are tagged, at parental request, for restricted use of certain library materials and data services. Frightened librarians are limiting young students to the "easy" books section, and they are requiring older students to bring written parental permission to read such books as Judy Blume's *Forever*, Katherine Paterson's *Bridge to Terabithia*, Mark Twain's *Huckleberry Finn*, Harper Lee's *To Kill a Mockingbird*, Alice Walker's *The Color Purple*, J. K. Rowling's Harry Potter books, and Maya Angelou's *I Know Why the Caged Bird Sings*. Some libraries are limiting children and young adults to preselected Internet sites. Professionals are self-censoring in the selection process—making every effort to make "safe" choices. These practices, however, aren't eliminating the problem; they are only amplifying the issue.

The problem is obvious. Censors want to control the minds of the young. They are fearful of the educational system, because students who read learn to think. Thinkers learn to see. Those who see often question. And, young people who question threaten the "blind" and the "non-thinkers." The answer is the classroom. As educators, we cannot, for the sake of the students, allow ourselves to be bullied into diluting the curriculum into superficial facts. We must talk about the principles of intellectual freedom. We must challenge students to think about the intent of our forefathers when they wrote the Bill of Rights. We must teach students about their First Amendment rights rather than restrict their use of particular books and materials. As educators, we must encourage students to express their own opinions while respecting the views of others.

By eighth grade, most students can define the Bill of Rights. They can, in a poetic fashion, render a memorized definition of the First Amendment. But, do they really know how it affects their lives? Experience tells me that they don't. Teachers, through interdisciplinary units of study, can lead students toward understanding the implications of the First Amendment for all Americans. As librarians and library media specialists, we must realize that our task is much broader than raising public consciousness for First Amendment rights through Banned Books Week exhibits. Our professional role extends beyond removing all restrictions and barriers from the library collection. We must do these things, but we must also accept responsibility for creating a vital connection between the social studies and English curricula by preparing lessons on the First Amendment. We can go into the classroom and engage students in activities and discussion that will enable them to think about their personal rights and responsibilities provided by the Constitution. The appropriate time to make this connection is when students are already engaged in a study of the Constitution. Ask students to read and react to a contemporary young adult novel such as Richard Peck's *The Last Safe Place on Earth*, Julian Thompson's *The Trials of Molly Sheldon*, or Stephanie Tolan's *Save Halloween*, that deals with censorship issues. Invite them to apply the situations in the novel to real life. Encourage them to debate the conflict presented in each novel. Ask them to read the short stories in *Places I Never Meant to Be*, edited by Judy Blume. Then, have them discuss how censorship has affected the writing careers of writers like David Klass, Norma Klein, Julius Lester, Chris Lynch, Harry Mazer, Norma Fox Mazer, Walter Dean Myers, Katherine Paterson, Susan Beth Pfeffer, Rachel Vail, Jacqueline Woodson, and Paul Zindel. Allow students time to research various First Amendment issues, whether it be book censorship, Internet filtering, or school journalism. Provide a forum in which students can express their views regarding the subject of intellectual freedom. And, help them understand their personal options regarding the use of books and materials that might offend them. Above all, grant them the opportunity to think, to speak, and to be heard. Classrooms and schools that foster this type of open atmosphere are sending a clear message: the First Amendment is important in school as well as in society at large. Thinkers, regardless of their views, make an important contribution to the American way of life. And, thinkers are less likely to become censors.

SETTING THE SCENE

- Make available copies of the First and Fourteenth Amendments so that the class can read them. Ask the students to discuss what the First Amendment means to them. What would happen to our society if all ideas were censored? At what point does one relinquish one's First Amendment rights? How are the First and Fourteenth Amendments related?

- Display the following books: Maurice Sendak's *Where the Wild Things Are*, William Steig's *Sylvester and the Magic Pebble*, Carolivia Herron's *Nappy Hair*, Judy Blume's *Are You There, God? It's Me, Margaret*, Lois Lowry's *The Giver*, Phyllis Naylor's *Shiloh*, Christopher Paul Curtis's *The Watsons Go to Birmingham–1963*, J. K. Rowling's Harry Potter books, and Paul Zindel's *The Pigman*. Ask students how many of them have read these books. Then, ask them to identify reasons why some people find these titles objectionable. Solicit answers to the following: How does banning these books violate your First Amendment rights? What would you say to someone who told you that one of these titles was inappropriate for you to read? What can you do to protect your First Amendment rights?

DISCUSSION

- Discuss the difference between a book challenge and censorship.
- How would your life be affected if we didn't have the First Amendment?
- Explain the following statement: Every time we listen to another person's opinion, we are supporting the principles of intellectual freedom.
- Censorship is really about gaining "power" and "control" over what others believe and think. Organized religious groups bring many book challenges. Why does this happen? Why did our forefathers feel it necessary to include an amendment to the Constitution that guarantees freedom of religion to all Americans? Discuss the relationship between freedom of religion and freedom of expression.
- Explain the following quote by John Morley: "You have not converted a man because you have silenced him." How is book censorship an attempt to "silence" the writer and the reader?
- In the *Pico* censorship case (1982), one school board member said, "I would not dream of trying to take that book out of the public library. That would be censorship—and we are not censors." What are your feelings regarding this statement? Why would he think that removing a book from the school library would not be censorship? How is the mission of a school library similar to that of a public library? How is it different?

- Interpret the following quote by Oscar Wilde: "The books that the world calls immoral are the books that show the world its own shame."

- In some cities, there is a movement to place ratings on books in school and public libraries. These ratings would be similar to the ones placed on movies and music. How are ratings on any work of art a form of censorship? How do you respond when you see that something is R rated? Does it enhance your curiosity? What is it about human nature that makes us want to read the books that a person forbids us to read? Suggest ways that a family can deal with controversial books, movies, Internet sites, and music without forbidding their use.

- What is the meaning of "academic freedom"? Why is it important that educational institutions maintain this freedom?

- Technological advances have brought about new issues regarding censorship and intellectual freedom. How does the First Amendment protect user rights on the Internet and other online services? When "surfing the Net," it is possible that you will come upon a conversation or graphics that offend you. How should you handle such a situation? Should online services be controlled or monitored for children? Why or why not?

- Elements and topics in books and movies that are often the targets of censors are profanity, racism, violence, magic and witchcraft, and sex. Some people believe that books with these elements provide "bad" role models for young readers. How might reading these books allow readers the opportunity to better understand these elements in our society and to discuss ways to deal with them?

ACTIVITIES

- Alvin Schwartz's *Scary Stories to Tell in the Dark* has been among the top 10 most censored books in the United States today. Poll 25 adults, asking them if and why they feel scary stories are harmful to children and teenagers. Then, poll 25 of your peers, asking them the same question. Make a chart showing the results of each poll. What conclusions might be drawn from your survey?

- Some parents feel that Halloween promotes evil and should not be celebrated in schools. Research the origin of Halloween, and prepare a persuasive speech about why it should or should not be celebrated by children.

- Find out your school district's procedure for dealing with challenged books and materials. Invite a member of the materials review committee or a member of the school board to speak to your class about local challenges. Prepare questions for the speaker.

- Read *Annie on My Mind* by Nancy Garden. Then, use the Internet to research the censorship case that occurred with Garden's book in Olathe, Kansas. High school students played a significant role in "Saving Annie" by asking the courts to force the school superintendent to return *Annie on My Mind* to the library shelves of their high school. How is Garden's book about discrimination? How is the Kansas censorship case about discrimination? Write a short paper that draws a parallel between the actions of the school administrators in the novel and those of the Olathe school superintendent.

- Research the purpose of each of the following organizations: the American Library Association's Office for Intellectual Freedom, the American Civil Liberties Union, the National Coalition against Censorship, the First Amendment Congress, and People for the American Way. Make brochures describing the mission of each organization. Include mailing addresses, Internet addresses, and telephone numbers. Display the brochures in the school library.

- Read Ray Bradbury's *Fahrenheit 451* and Lois Lowry's *The Giver*. Write a paper discussing how each book represents thought control.

- Research Justice William Joseph Brennan's contribution to the *Pico* censorship case. Justice Brennan retired from the Supreme Court on July 20, 1990, and died in 1997. Write a tribute to him from the "schoolchildren of America."

- Make a list of various types of censorship. Then, draw a political cartoon regarding one type.

- Using a periodical index or the Internet, locate as many articles as you can about book challenges in schools in the United States in the past five years. Draw a map of the United States and color in the states where you found challenges. Which state has the most challenges? How has each case been resolved?

- Ballads and legends are often written about heroic people. Research John Peter Zenger's historic fight for freedom of the press, and write a ballad or a legend about him (see Stephen Krensky's book in the bibliography).

- Banned Books Week is celebrated every September. The purpose of this observance is to make the public aware of the "horrors" and "harms" of censorship. Find out the dates of this special week, and create a Banned Books exhibit for the school.

FICTION CONNECTIONS

Christian, Peggy. *The Bookstore Mouse.* Illustrated by Gary A. Lippincott. 1995. 128p. Harcourt.

AGES 9–12   Cervantes, a mouse who lives in an antiquarian bookstore, embarks on a great adventure while trying to elude Milo the cat. When Cervantes discovers the power of words, he finds a special way to deal with Milo, and they both live a more enlightened life.

Diaz, Jorge. *The Rebellious Alphabet.* Illustrated by Ivind S. Jorfald. 1993. 32p. Holt.

AGES 8–12   For older readers, this illustrated fable tells the story of an illiterate dictator who bans reading and writing but is outwitted by an old man who trains canaries to deliver printed messages to people.

Facklam, Margery. *The Trouble with Mothers.* 1989. 160p. Clarion.

AGES 11–13   Eighth-grader Luke Troy is devastated when his mother, a teacher, writes a historical novel that is considered pornography by some people in the community where they live.

Garden, Nancy. *The Year They Burned the Books.* 1999. 256p. Farrar, Straus & Giroux.

AGES 12–UP   Jamie Crawford, the new editor of her high school newspaper, sets off an explosive controversy in her small New England town when she writes a feature article about a sex education curriculum and the distribution of condoms in her high school.

Hentoff, Nat. *The Day They Came to Arrest the Book.* 1983. 160p. Dell.

AGES 12–UP   Students in a high school English class protest the study of Mark Twain's *Huckleberry Finn* until the editor of the school newspaper uncovers other cases of censorship and, in a public hearing, reveals the truth behind the mysterious disappearance of certain library books and the resignation of the school librarian. Also note the 1988 film of the same name from Ruby-Spears Production—no longer distributed but possibly available in local film libraries.

Hewett, Lorri. *Lives of Our Own.* 1998. 214p. Dutton.

AGES 12–UP   Shawna, a new girl in town, faces resentment from class-mates when she writes a controversial article for the school newspaper about the traditional Old South Ball.

Krensky, Stephen. *The Printer's Apprentice.* Illustrated by Madeline Sorel. 1995. 112p. Delacorte.

AGES 10–13   Using John Peter Zenger, a 1700s New York newspaper publisher, as his focus, Krensky unfolds a story about a young appren-tice who witnesses the dramatic trial that changed the course of American journalism.

Lasky, Kathryn. *Memoirs of a Bookbat.* 1994. 192p. Harcourt.

AGES 12–14   Harper Jessup, an avid reader, runs away because she feels that her individual rights are threatened when her parents, born-again fundamentalists, lodge a public promotion of book censorship.

Meyer, Carolyn. *Drummers of Jericho.* 1995. 336p. Harcourt.

AGES 12–14   When a 14-year-old Jewish girl joins the high school march-ing band and discovers that the band will play hymns and stand in the formation of a cross, she objects, raising major issues of individual rights.

Miles, Betty. *Maudie and Me and the Dirty Book.* 1980. 144p. Knopf.

AGES 8–11   Eleven-year-old Kate Harris volunteers to read to first-graders, but her choice of book, *The Birthday Dog,* causes the children to ask questions about how puppies are born. When parents of the younger children raise an objection, the principal suspends the reading project, and Kate and her friends learn about censorship firsthand.

Neufeld, John. *A Small Civil War.* 1996. 182p. Atheneum.

AGES 12–UP   At 13, Georgia Van Buren fights the banning of *The Grapes of Wrath* in her school library, but is dismayed and shocked when her family disagrees with her stand.

Peck, Richard. *The Last Safe Place on Earth.* 1995. 161p. Delacorte.

AGES 11–14   The Tobin family is satisfied that Walden Woods is a quiet, safe community to rear three children. Then, seven-year-old Marnie begins having nightmares after a teenage baby-sitter tells her that Halloween is evil, and Todd and Diana, sophomores in high school, witness an organized group's attempt to censor books in their school library.

Thompson, Julian F. *The Trials of Molly Sheldon*. 1995. 150p. Holt.

AGES 12–UP   When high schooler Molly Sheldon begins working for her father in his eclectic general store in central Vermont, she, for the first time in her life, faces First Amendment issues. Moralists try to censor the books that her father sells, and Molly is accused of being a witch.

Tolan, Stephanie S. *Save Halloween!* 1993. 176p. Morrow.

AGES 10–13   Sixth-grader Johnna Filkings gets caught up in researching and writing a class pageant about Halloween; much to her dismay, her father and uncle, fundamentalist ministers, disrupt the entire community by declaring Halloween evil.

NONFICTION CONNECTIONS

Faber, Doris and Harold. *We the People: The Story of the United States Constitution since 1787*. 1987. 256p. Scribner.

AGES 11–13   A historical account of the writing of the Constitution and the adoption of the Bill of Rights, including a discussion of the responsibility of the Supreme Court as an interpreter of this important document.

Gold, John C. *Board of Education vs. Pico*. 1994. 96p. Twenty-First Century Books.

AGES 11–UP   Gold traces the Pico case from its beginning in 1975 to the 1982 final Supreme Court decision that ordered the school board of the Island Trees Union Free School District No. 26 on Long Island, New York, to return nine books to the library shelves.

Greenberg, Keith. *Adolescent Rights: Are Young People Equal under the Law?* 1995. 64p. Holt/Twenty-First Century Books.

AGES 11–UP   Greenberg details adolescent rights from both historical and contemporary perspectives, and invites readers to form their own conclusions regarding specific issues.

Hentoff, Nat. *The First Freedom: The Tumultuous History of Free Speech in America*. 1988. 363p. Delacorte.

AGES 12–UP   In this revised edition, Hentoff discusses the history of free speech in America and deals specifically with related controversial issues in the latter part of the twentieth century.

Herda, D. J. *New York Times v. United States: National Security and Censorship*. 1994. 104p. Enslow.

AGES 11–UP   Herda explores the 1971 landmark decision in which the Supreme Court decided in favor of the right of the *New York Times* to publish articles about the U.S. government's "secret war" against Vietnam and Cambodia.

Kronenwetter, Michael. *Under 18: Knowing Your Rights*. 1993. 112p. Enslow.

AGES 11–UP   Focusing primarily on young people's rights while they are at school, this book also examines how these rights can best be established and protected.

Lang, Susan S. and Paul Lang. *Censorship*. 1993. 126p. Watts.

AGES 10–13   This overview of censorship topics presents issues for discussion, such as cigarette advertising and rap lyrics.

Leone, Bruno, ed. *Free Speech*. 1994. 236p. Greenhaven Press.

AGES 11–UP   Featuring articles that deal with all types of free speech issues, this book debates particular topics, such as censorship, pornography, and libel.

Meltzer, Milton. *The Bill of Rights: How We Got It and What It Means*. 1990. 180p. HarperCollins.

AGES 11–15   This comprehensive discussion of the history of the Bill of Rights gives specific references to contemporary challenges against these 10 amendments.

Monroe, Judy. *Censorship*. 1990. 48p. Crestwood House.

AGES 10–12   A short, basic overview, in simple language, of the problems of censorship with regard to textbooks, movies, music, and children's books.

Nardo, Don. *The Bill of Rights.* 1998. 128p. Greenhaven Press. Opposing Viewpoints Digests

AGES 12–UP   Focuses on the historical debates regarding the need for a bill of rights, and presents later debates about various individual rights issues.

Netzley, Patricia D. *Issues in Censorship.* 2000. 80p. Lucent. Contemporary Issues

AGES 9–11   An overview of issues related to censorship, including a discussion about hate speech and book banning.

Pascoe, Elaine. *Freedom of Expression: The Right to Speak Out in America.* 1992. 128p. Millbrook.

AGES 10–13   Pascoe supplies a variety of historical and contemporary issues related to the First Amendment.

Rappaport, Doreen. *Tinker vs. Des Moines: Student Rights on Trial.* 1993. 160p. HarperCollins.

AGES 12–UP   Part of the Be the Judge/Be the Jury series, this book deals with First and Fourteenth Amendment rights by re-creating the trial of John Tinker and his classmates, who were suspended from school in 1965 for protesting the Vietnam War by wearing black armbands.

Steele, Philip. *Censorship.* 1992. 48p. New Discovery Books.

AGES 10–13   This short, seven-chapter book looks at the history of censorship and its impact on American society.

Steins, Richard. *Censorship: How Does It Conflict with Freedom?* 1995. 64p. Holt/Twenty-First Century Books.

AGES 11–13   The complex issue of censorship and how it affects and threatens our lives is addressed from historical and contemporary perspectives.

Zeinert, Karen. *Free Speech: From Newspapers to Music Lyrics.* 1995. 128p. Enslow.

AGES 12–UP   By introducing cases involving young people and then surveying what has happened with such issues in the past, Zeinert places today's censorship battles in a historical context.

STRATEGY 2

Places I Never Meant to Be

Original Stories by Censored Writers

Simon & Schuster   1999   198 pages

Edited by JUDY BLUME

AGES 12–UP

Those of us who oppose censorship believe that reading about some-thing is a safe way to explore and understand it, and that is the best way to prepare young people to deal with the issues they will face, both in school and later in life.

— Joan Bertin, Executive Director,
National Coalition against Censorship

Young adults making tough decisions about life and the importance of communication are the underlying themes that unite these 12 short stories by well-known writers of young adult fiction. Like in real life, these adolescent characters find themselves in unintended situations. There is a mugging, a fire that may have been set by a teenager, an adult bully at a baseball camp, an infatuation with a teacher. There is a homeless boy's need for a family, a teenager's first experience with sex, and a boy who learns the real meaning

---

This strategy has been adapted from a *Reading Group Guide* prepared by the author for Simon and Schuster.

of bigotry. The writers of these stories never compromise the truth. Their stories are honest and faithful to the emotions of the growing adolescent. And, they celebrate their genuine respect for their readers by becoming the guiding force behind free expression for children and young adults in this nation.

In "Meeting the Mugger" by Norma Fox Mazer, 15-year-old Sarabeth feels that she doesn't need the constant advice that her mother seems determined to give. The sex talks are the worst. Her mom wants to make sure that Sarabeth understands "safe sex" and doesn't end up pregnant at 16 as she did. One night during one of these talks, Sarabeth runs from the house and comes face-to-face with a female mugger. Later, Sarabeth relates the story to her friends at school: "It's the worst thing that ever happened to me. Not losing my jacket, not even being cut, but being helpless, at the mercy of someone else." In many ways, the mugging is a life-changing experience for Sarabeth, and she begins to understand her mother's need to give advice. When her mother is diagnosed with cancer and dies, Sarabeth finally realizes that her mother was only trying to keep her safe, because eventually we are all "mugged in life."

"Spear" by Julius Lester deals with overt racism when Norma Jean Ray, a white girl, enrolls in an African American literature class and meets head-on with immense hostility from the all-black class. "Hey, you! White girl! You sure you in the right class?" When the hurtful remarks continue, Spear, the son of "Black Spear," a slain black leader involved in race riots in the 1970s, steps in to defend her. Spear and Norma Jean discover that they have something in common—they are both products of racist parents, and they both understand the meaning of bigotry. Norma Jean eventually drops the class, Spear denounces his father's past and makes a life-changing move toward anonymity by taking his given name, Adrian, and refusing to accompany his mother on speaking engagements.

Rachel Vail tells the story of a teenage couple's first sexual experience in "Going Sentimental." Jody and Mackey have been friends since elementary school and a couple since seventh grade. Now, in high school, the two athletes decide that they are old enough for sex. Jody, a star on the girl's basketball team, isn't sure about the experience after it's over. "What does it mean if you feel nothing much, after?" Left to ponder the question of love, romance, and passion, Jody knows that she will never forget losing her virginity, and neither will Mackey.

Set in Japan, "The Red Dragonfly" by Katherine Paterson tells of a young boy's infatuation with his teacher. "She was like the red dragonfly of the late summer, delicate herald of autumn, precursor of the year's loveliness." He writes a poem for her and delivers it to her home, only to discover that there is a man in her life.

"July Saturday" by Jacqueline Woodson is told in first person from a young girl's point of view and takes place in a "middle to upper-class" neighborhood where the children play together and the mamas visit over coffee in their kitchens. One day a neighbor's house burns to the ground, and the firemen suspect arson. No one knows who might have started the fire, but a teenage girl hanging back and watching is the obvious suspect. As the neighbors gather to offer support to the now homeless Williams family, the narrator and her friend, Claytena Smalls, spot the teenager talking in a rather familiar way to Mr. Williams. The events of the day are tough to understand, and the girls begin to realize that they are growing up and that the carefree days of their childhood are left to memory.

Aaron Hill, the main character in Harry Mazer's "You Come, Too, A-Ron," is sent to Oakmont, a state school for homeless and troubled teenagers, after his mother throws a knife at him and is committed to a mental hospital. Aaron can't seem to adjust to Oakmont and turns himself into Placement in hopes of finding another place to live. But, teenagers are tough to place. What Aaron isn't prepared for is the role he might play in the life of Kenny, a little boy he meets at Placement. Aaron plans to take to the streets rather than return to Oakmont until he realizes that at Oakmont he can stay in touch with Kenny by telephone, and maybe even take him to the park as he had promised.

In "The Beast Is in the Labyrinth" by Walter Dean Myers, 17-year-old John is one of the few black students at a small college in Millersville, Pennsylvania. He had been anxious to get away from the streets and the people that he knew in his Harlem neighborhood, so when he won a scholarship to college, he felt that this was his chance. John does return home for holidays, often finding his sister Timmi "sick" from drugs and his mother sick with worry. These trips home cause him to ponder the difficult questions that the TA from school has posed. "Where is home?. . . Is it where the heart is, or from whence the soul has sprung?" When Timmi dies, John realizes that he must have appeared a stranger to his sister because they had certainly taken different routes in the maze of life.

Susan Beth Pfeffer's main character in "Ashes" is faced with a tough decision when her father gets into a financial predicament and appeals to Ashleigh, whom he calls Ashes, to help him out. On one of her weekly visits with him, he describes his situation and asks her to take two hundred dollars stored in the teapot in her mother's kitchen. Ashes enters the kitchen and looks into the teapot. "Mom's emergency money. Her earthquake money. Her Martian money. Ten Andrew Jacksons stared right back to me. They offered me no advice on what I should do."

In "Baseball Camp" by David Klass, Eric attends a baseball camp for teenagers and quickly learns that bullies aren't always kids. Paul Creese, the coach, curses the boys, beats up on them, and shouts verbal insults at them. "Not one of you's got a lick of talent and you're each uglier than a rat-eared mongrel dog." Roger, the son of a big-shot lawyer, decides that he has had enough and reports Creese to the camp authorities. The coach is fired, but just before he leaves, he calls the team together and addresses them, "Boys, I have some sad news. We have a squealer in the camp."

Tuesday, the teenage main character in Paul Zindel's "Love and Centipedes," has had an extraordinary week. It began when she was assigned Kyle Ecneps, Maureen Willoughby's boyfriend, as a partner for a science project. The two meet to work on the project, and Tuesday finds herself falling in love with Kyle. One must wonder about Maureen's motive when she asks Tuesday to help out with the prom committee. When Maureen comes to Tuesday's house and discovers Kyle's ankle brace on Tuesday's arm, the two end up in a tragic fight.

"Lie, No Lie" by Chris Lynch is the story of two unlikely friends. "We make no sense to anybody but ourselves. We are the wrong people for each other, nothing alike, but somehow we fill each other in and have done so for all of time—kindergarten, grade school and now." When Pauly takes Oakley to a gym and a guy hits up on him, Oakley tells Pauly that he doesn't like the joke. Pauly simply says that he thought he was doing Oakley a favor. At this moment, Oakley becomes determined to hurt Pauly and tells him that he has slept with his girlfriend. Pauly responds, "Next time can you let me know. . . so I can watch."

The final story in this collection is "Something Which Is Non-existent" by the late Norma Klein. Ben and Michael meet in the Music Room on the college campus where they are students, and agree to study together in Michael's room in an effort to escape the "bohemian atmosphere" of the Music Room. Their growing friendship takes a turn when Michael begins going out with a girl from his Modern Novel class. Though girls try to lure Ben, he isn't interested. Instead he writes a "two-page treatise on friendship" and then declares it "the biggest piece of baloney he had ever read."

SETTING THE SCENE

Places I Never Meant to Be has a twofold purpose—to help young adults understand the meaning of censorship and to benefit the National Coalition against Censorship. Ask students to define censorship. Have the class prepare a survey that includes the following questions:

1. What is the First Amendment?
2. What is censorship?
3. What is intellectual freedom?

Ask students to survey 10 adults, using the questionnaire they prepared in class. Then have students share the results of their survey. What does the survey reveal about public knowledge regarding the First Amendment, censorship, and intellectual freedom? Read aloud "A Letter from Joan Bertin, Executive Director of the National Coalition against Censorship." Discuss the purpose of and the need for such an organization.

DISCUSSION

- Judy Blume states in "A Personal View" that her desire to read *A Rage to Live* by John O'Hara grew when she was forbidden to read it. How do the words *forbidden* and *restricted* enhance a person's curiosity? How do ratings on films affect your desire to see them?

- Communication is a common theme in young adult literature. It is the lack of communication that sometimes causes censorship. Why is it important to talk about issues with your family and friends? Discuss the underlying theme of communication in each of the short stories in this book. Which character suffers most from a lack of communication? What is wrong with the way Paul Creese communicates in "Baseball Camp" by David Klass? How does Roger communicate the thoughts of all the campers? How does his willingness to speak up affect the other characters and the outcome of the story? What does Norma Fox Mazer mean when she says, "Censorship is crippling, negating, stifling"? How is an unwillingness to communicate "crippling, negating, and stifling"? How does the intent of the First Amendment encourage and support communication?

- Katherine Paterson says that teachers and librarians who stand up to censors are heroic. Discuss the qualities of a hero. How does it take courag... ... ...ro? How does Adrian in "Spear" by Julius Lester ...compare and contrast Adrian's courage to that ... Norma, the white girl in the African American ...ow courage? What does she teach Adrian? How is ...of communicating his beliefs similar to the way book ...ate their beliefs? Why does it take more courage to ...in a peaceful manner?

I made a vow to myself when I was a teenager that I ...t, and never disrespect, the intensity of the adoles- ...Discuss what Vail means by the "adolescent experi- ...Vail show respect for the "adolescent experience" in ...al"? How do the writers of the short stories in this ...trate an understanding of young adult emotions and ...dolescent experience"? How is censorship about dis- ...intellectual freedom promote respect?

- Discuss what Harry Mazer means when he says, "Books are our windows on the world." Which of the short stories most represents your thoughts and feelings? Which of the stories opens your mind to other ways of life? Katherine Paterson writes about another culture in "The Red Dragonfly." How does she reveal that the adolescent emotion of love and infatuation is universal? Why is it important to read about other cultures and to explore the way other people think? Why are censors threatened by diversity?

- What does Chris Lynch mean when he says, "Challenge me? I challenge you back"? How does this statement reflect what the First Amendment is about? How can intellectual challenge result in a healthy debate?

- The late Norma Klein once stated, "I still can't believe there's anything objectionable about telling it like it is." All the contributors to this short story collection believe that censorship stifles the "truth." Discuss why censors are so frightened by "truth." How does each short story in this collection reflect the writers' commitment to telling the "truth"?

- In each of these stories, the young adult main character must make an important decision. Compare and contrast Jon's decision in "The Beast Is in the Labyrinth" by Walter Dean Myers to the decision Ashleigh makes in "Ashes" by Susan Beth Pfeffer. How do the decisions they make affect themselves and their families? One is often faced with tough decisions in life. How does intellectual freedom support and promote the ability to make tough decisions?

ACTIVITIES

- Judy Blume tried to get John O'Hara's book A *Rage to Live* from the public library when she was a teenager, but was told she would need parental permission in writing. Find out the policies of the public library in your town or city regarding young adults' access to the adult collection. Write an editorial for the newspaper either defending or opposing the policies of the public library.

- David Klass says, "There is no way I can truthfully render characters if I must constantly worry about offending censors." Select a passage from either "Baseball Camp" by David Klass or "Lie, No Lie" by Chris Lynch that might offend someone. Then, rewrite the passage, omitting the offensive parts. How do these omissions change the characters? How does it change the message of the story? Why is "truth" in characters essential to a good story?

- What is the importance of the First Amendment? Discuss the relationship between the First and the Fourteenth Amendments. Research one of the following court cases: *Tinker vs. Des Moines School District* (1969), *Board of Education, Island Trees Union Free School District No. 26 vs. Pico* (1982), *Hazelwood School District vs. Kuhlmeier* (1988). What do these cases have to do with free expression? What do they reveal about students' rights?

- Margaret Mead once stated, "Thanks to television, for the first time the young are seeing history made before it is censored by their elders." Find out what parts of our history have been censored. Debate the value of television in reporting history as it is happening. How do the news media sensationalize the events they report? Select a local, national, or world event, and view the news coverage of that event on one of the major television networks. In class, compare and contrast the way the event is covered by the different networks. Why is it important to gather information from several sources before forming an opinion regarding past or present history? How does ignorance promote censorship?

- One of the most well-known censorship cases in the United States was the Scopes Trial. Research this case, and discuss how the issue of evolution remains a volatile subject among some people. What other areas of science might provoke a form of censorship? How does the advancement of science require intellectual and free thought? Debate whether the government has the right to enforce health regulations on people like the Christian Scientists who do not believe in medical treatment. How might this be viewed as a First Amendment issue?

- One of the current issues regarding free speech is young adult access to the Internet. Ask at least 15 adults and 15 teenagers whether young adults should have free and unrestricted access, limited access, or no access to the Internet. Using the data from the surveys, construct a graph that reveals public opinion regarding this issue.

- Using pictures from magazines and newspapers, create a poster collage that interprets the meaning of the First Amendment.

- Judy Blume is one of the most censored writers in America. Stage a talk show featuring a parental challenge to one of her books. Include a host who gives an introduction to the book and an overview of the challenge, parents who oppose the book, parents who support the book, a school or public library official who defends the book, and several young adults who have read the book. Allow students in the audience to ask questions and make comments.

BOOKS BY CONTRIBUTING WRITERS

Blume, Judy. *Are You There God? It's Me, Margaret.* 1970. 149p. Bradbury Press.

AGES 9–12   Twelve-year-old Margaret is approaching adolescence and is curious about menstruation and developing breasts. The product of Jewish-Protestant parents, she is also questioning religion and wondering which faith she will choose.

Blume, Judy. *Blubber.* 1974. 153p. Bradbury Press.

AGES 9–12   When overweight Linda makes a class oral report on whales, her fifth-grade classmates nickname her Blubber, setting off several incidents of class bullying.

Blume, Judy. *Deenie.* 1973. 159p. Bradbury Press.

AGES 10–12   Deenie is 12 years old and on the brink of a modeling career when her doctor discovers that she has curvature of the spine. This problem, coupled with questions regarding sex and sexuality, makes Deenie look at her life and friendships a little differently.

Blume, Judy. *Here's to You, Rachel Robinson*. 1993. 196p. Orchard Books.

AGES 11–14   Rachel Robinson, a gifted seventh-grader, is tormented by her older brother who is back home after being expelled from boarding school. (A companion novel to *Just As Long As We're Together*.)

Blume, Judy. *Then Again, Maybe I Won't*. 1971. 164p. Bradbury Press.

AGES 12–UP   When he is almost 13 years old, Tony Miglione moves to a new town, wonders about making new friends, and suddenly worries about his own physical maturation.

Blume, Judy. *Tiger Eyes*. 1981. 206p. Bradbury Press.

AGES 12–UP   Davey Wexler, along with her mother and brother, goes to visit a relative in Los Alamos, New Mexico, after the tragic murder of her father in a 7-Eleven store and meets a young man who helps her conquer her fears and deal with her grief.

Klass, David. *California Blue*. 1994. 200p. Scholastic.

AGES 12–UP   Seventeen-year-old John Rodgers finds himself in conflict with his dying father over an environmental issue that may affect the mill where his father works.

Klass, David. *Danger Zone*. 1996. 240p. Scholastic.

AGES 12–UP   Jimmy, a high school basketball star, is invited to play on a "Teen Dream Team" and travel to Italy to play in a tournament. He finds himself in the middle of a dramatic and suspenseful adventure when he encounters trouble with the local people.

Klass, David. *A Different Season*. 1988. 199p. Lodestar Books.

AGES 12–UP   Jim, the ace pitcher of his high school baseball team, is attracted to the school's best female athlete, but conflicts develop when he opposes her efforts to play on the boy's team.

Lester, Julius. *Long Journey Home: Stories from Black History*. 1998. 160p. Puffin Books.

AGES 12–UP   Six stories about slaves and ex-slaves that capture the essence of black history.

Lester, Julius. *This Strange New Feeling*. 1987. 176p. Scholastic/Point.

AGES 12–UP   A collection of three short stories about slavery and freedom.

Lester, Julius. *To Be a Slave*. Illustrated by Tom Feelings. 1998. 168p. Dial.

AGES 12–UP   A commentary about all the aspects of slavery told from the point of view of black men and women who had been slaves.

Lynch, Chris. *Extreme Elvin*. 1999. 240p. HarperCollins.

AGES 12–UP   Elvin Bishop, the antihero of *Slot Machine,* has survived summer camp and is preparing to tackle high school and all the horrors that come with it.

Lynch, Chris. *Gypsy Davey*. 1994. 179p. HarperCollins.

AGES 12–UP   Life is tough for fatherless, 12-year-old Davey, who finds himself the man of the house, caring for his mother and older sister, and now his sister's baby.

Lynch, Chris. *Iceman*. 1994. 181p. HarperCollins.

AGES 12–UP   Eric, a 14-year-old ice hockey player, is encouraged by his father to be vicious on the ice while his mother, a former nun, struggles to save his soul.

Lynch, Chris. *Shadow Boxer*. 1993. 215p. HarperCollins.

AGES 12–UP   After his father, a heavyweight boxer, dies, George feels responsible for his younger brother, Monty, and tries to steer him away from the rough life of the inner city where they live.

Lynch, Chris. *Whitechurch*. 1999. 192p. HarperCollins.

AGES 12–UP   Set in a small town, these stories tell of three friends— two teenage boys and a girl—and what happens when their friendship begins to fall apart.

Mazer, Harry. *I Love You, Stupid!* 1981. 185p. Crowell.

AGES 12–UP   At 17, Marcus doesn't admit that he is a virgin to anyone except Wendy who agrees to have sex with him just for the experience. A funny and entertaining coming-of-age story.

Mazer, Harry. *The Last Mission*. 1979. 182p. Delacorte.

AGES 12–UP   A 15-year-old Jewish boy lies about his age to enlist in the United States Air Corps during World War II and is taken prisoner by the Germans.

Mazer, Harry. *When the Phone Rang.* 1985. 181p. Scholastic.

AGES 12–UP   Three siblings struggle to keep their family together when their parents are killed in a plane crash.

Mazer, Norma Fox. *After the Rain.* 1987. 291p. Morrow.

AGES 12–UP   Fifteen-year-old Rachel, who is on the verge of womanhood, and Izzy, her dying grandfather, teach one another important lessons about life, love, and family.

Mazer, Norma Fox. *Dear Bill, Remember Me? And Other Stories.* 1978. 208p. Dell.

AGES 12–UP   These short stories present eight young women who are seeking independence, self-confidence, and relationships with young men while dealing with family issues, such as alcoholism and serious illness.

Mazer, Norma Fox. *Silver.* 1988. 261p. Morrow.

AGES 12–UP   Fourteen-year-old Sarabeth Silver lives in a trailer with her mother, but when she transfers to a school where most of the girls are rich and pretty, she finds out that looks can be deceiving and that there can be painful secrets even among the more affluent.

Mazer, Norma Fox. *Taking Terri Mueller.* 1983, c1981. 221p. Morrow.

AGES 12–UP   Terri Mueller has lived with the belief that her mother was killed in a car accident until she overhears a conversation that reveals that she was kidnapped by her father and that her mother is still alive.

Mazer, Norma Fox. *Up in Seth's Room.* 1979. 199p. Delacorte.

AGES 12–UP   When 15-year-old Finn meets 19-year-old Seth, she finds herself in a bitter conflict when he makes sexual demands and she realizes that she isn't ready.

Mazer, Norma Fox. *When She Was Good.* 1997. 240p. Scholastic.

AGES 12–UP   A gripping story about 14-year-old Em Thurkill who grows up with the rage of an alcoholic father, the silence of a frightened mother, and unrelenting abuse from a mentally ill older sister.

Myers, Walter Dean. *Fallen Angels.* 1988. 309p. Scholastic.

AGES 12–UP   Seventeen-year-old Richie Perry relates the horror and fear he experienced during his tour of duty in Vietnam with the United States military in the late 1960s.

Myers, Walter Dean. *Fast Sam, Cool Clyde, and Stuff.* 1975. 190p. Viking.

AGES 11-14   Stuff, now 18 years old, remembers the year that he was 13 and the gang that he hung out with on 116th Street.

Myers, Walter Dean. *Hoops: A Novel.* 1981. 183p. Delacorte.

AGES 11-13   Seventeen-year-old Lonnie believes that basketball is his ticket out of the troubled streets of his Harlem neighborhood.

Myers, Walter Dean. *Monster.* 1999. 279p. HarperCollins.

AGES 12-UP   In the form of a film script, 16-year-old Steve Harmon relates his experiences in prison and in the courtroom where he is on trial as an accomplice to a murder.

Myers, Walter Dean. *Scorpions.* 1988. 216p. Harper & Row.

AGES 11-13   Jamal Hicks, age 12, becomes the leader of the Scorpions, a gang in his Harlem neighborhood, and, through a tragedy, learns important lessons about friendship and the consequences of owning a gun.

Myers, Walter Dean. *Somewhere in the Darkness.* 1992. 168p. Scholastic.

AGES 12-UP   Jimmy, a teenage boy who lives with his aunt in Harlem, accompanies Crab, his father, who has escaped from prison, on a trip to Arkansas and in the process learns a lot about his father's past and begins thinking about the true meaning of fatherhood.

Paterson, Katherine. *Bridge to Terabithia.* 1977. 128p. Crowell.

AGES 9-12   Ten-year-old Jess deals with the death of Leslie, a new friend who helped him create a special and magical hideaway that they called "Terabithia."

Paterson, Katherine. *The Great Gilly Hopkins.* 1978. 148p. Crowell.

AGES 10-12   Gilly Hopkins, an 11-year-old foster child, is against anyone who tries to be friendly until she is placed in the home of Maime Trotter, a fat and nearly illiterate widow, who teaches her about love and compassion.

Paterson, Katherine. *Jacob Have I Loved.* 1980. 216p. Crowell.

AGES 12-UP   Living in the 1940s on a small Chesapeake Bay island, Louise Bradshaw feels robbed of everything that is important to her: attention from her parents, hopes for an education off the island, and a relationship with Call, a childhood friend.

Pfeffer, Susan Beth. *About David*. 1980. 167p. Delacorte.

AGES 12–UP   Lynn is overwhelmed with unbelievable pain and grief as she deals with the fact that David, her 17-year-old friend, has murdered his parents and killed himself.

Pfeffer, Susan Beth. *A Matter of Principle: A Novel*. 1982. 181p. Delacorte.

AGES 12–UP   A group of high school students comes face-to-face with an important constitutional issue when the school's principal objects to an underground newspaper that they are publishing.

Pfeffer, Susan Beth. *The Year without Michael*. 1987. 164p. Bantam Books.

AGES 12–UP   Jody struggles to hold her family together as they deal with the sudden disappearance of her 13-year-old brother, Michael.

Vail, Rachel. *Daring to Be Abigail: A Novel*. 1996. 130p. Orchard Books.

AGES 9–11   A summer at Camp Nashaquitsa is the chance for 11-year-old Abigail to overcome being a coward, but when funny summer pranks turn into cruel acts against others, Abigail is faced with serious questions about who she wants to be.

Vail, Rachel. *Do-Over: A Novel*. 1992. 143p. Orchard Books.

AGES 11–13   Whitman, 13 years old and angry at his father for leaving his mother, faces the typical adolescent uncertainties regarding friends and self when he suddenly finds himself center stage in his first play.

Vail, Rachel. *Ever After: A Novel*. 1994. 166p. Orchard Books.

AGES 10–14   Fourteen-year-old Molly is about to enter high school and records all her thoughts and feelings about growing up in a journal, including her desire for a close friend, her worries about her appearance, and boys.

Woodson, Jacqueline. *From the Notebooks of Melanin Sun*. 1995. 160p. Scholastic/Blue Sky.

AGES 12–UP   When his mother begins a relationship with another woman, a 14-year-old boy must deal with his own fears and prejudices.

Woodson, Jacqueline. *I Hadn't Meant to Tell You This*. 1994. 115p. Delacorte.

AGES 12–UP   Marie, the only black girl in eighth grade, and Lena, a white classmate, are both motherless, only Lena harbors the terrible secret that her father is sexually abusing her.

Woodson, Jacqueline. *Miracle's Boys*. 2000. 133p. Putnam.

AGES 12–UP   The youngest of three orphaned brothers, Lafayette is blamed for their mother's death, and is worried about what will happen when Charlie, an older brother, is released from a detention home and comes home to stay. Can they stick together or will they be torn apart?

Zindel, Paul. *A Begonia for Miss Applebaum*. 1989. 180p. Harper & Row.

AGES 12–UP   When Miss Applebaum, a favorite teacher, becomes terminally ill with cancer, 15-year-old Henry and his friend Zelda are her constant companions and learn great lessons about humanity, courage, and death.

Zindel, Paul. *My Darling, My Hamburger: A Novel*. 1969. 168p. Harper & Row.

AGES 12–UP   Four troubled high school seniors who are desperate to be accepted among their peers become soul mates and find themselves caught between fear and the desire for intimacy.

Zindel, Paul. *The Pigman: A Novel*. 1968. 182p. Harper & Row.

AGES 12–UP   Two lonely teenagers befriend Mr. Pignati, an old man who collects ceramic pigs, and in the process learn lessons about responsible behavior.

Zindel, Paul. *The Pigman's Legacy*. 1980. 183p. Harper & Row.

AGES 12–UP   In this sequel to *The Pigman*, John and Lorraine deal with Mr. Pignati's death by befriending another old man

Zindel, Paul. *The Undertaker's Gone Bananas*. 1978. 239p. Harper & Row.

AGES 12–UP   In this zany novel, two teenagers are convinced that a neighbor, an undertaker, has killed his wife.

STRATEGY 3

Blubber

Bradbury Press   1974   153 pages

JUDY BLUME

AGES 10–12

I will act the same as always except I'll just ignore Wendy. That will teach her a lesson about threatening people.

—Jill Brenner, age 10, in *Blubber*

At 10 years old everyone needs a best friend, and most kids want to be part of a group. But, can the desire to be a part of the "popular crowd" be so strong that a person loses sight of what is right and wrong? Fifth-grader Jill Brenner is suddenly in the middle of this type of situation. At first, Jill is an innocent bystander, but when overweight Linda Fischer gives an oral report on whales, Wendy, the most popular girl in the class, passes a note to Caroline and then to Jill that says, "Blubber is a good name for her!" Mrs. Minish, the teacher, doesn't have complete control of the class and only makes idle threats about the girls' behavior. Then, on the school bus, another group of girls tortures Linda by singing "Blubbery blubber. . . blub, blub, blub, blub. . ." to the tune of "Beautiful Dreamer." Boys taunt her with words like "She won't need a coat this winter. She's got her blubber to keep her warm." Paper airplanes that say "I'm Blubber—Fly Me" soar from the rear of the school bus. At times, Jill shows signs of being uncomfortable with the way Linda is treated by her classmates, but her desire to please Wendy is just too strong, and she soon becomes a ringleader.

In the meantime, it's Halloween and the big event is the school Halloween Parade and costume contest. Jill is determined to win the contest for the most original costume, and decides to go as a flenser, a person who removes blubber from a whale. She paints her good boots gold, makes a cardboard sword, and at the last minute, prepares a sign that says FLENSER to wear around her neck. Is she really trying to be original, or is it just another way of making fun of Linda? Whatever her reason, Jill's flenser costume is unsuccessful, and Fred Yarmouth wins as a fried egg. Though Jill's costume doesn't get the attention of the judges, Wendy and her followers make great notice and appoint Jill, the flenser, the task of stripping Blubber of her clothing. The gang gathers in the girls' rest room and holds Blubber down while Jill attempts to undress her. Though the girls never accomplish their task, they do manage to reveal Linda's "flowered underpants" and prove that she does indeed wear an undershirt. Wendy, dressed as a queen, demands to be addressed as "Her Majesty" and orders Blubber to "Curtsy to the queen."

By now, the daily routine of the entire class is to make fun of Linda. There are jump rope rhymes that are so mean that Linda stays inside during recess to avoid the laughter.

> Oh, what a riot
>
> Blubber's on a diet
>
> I wonder what's the matter
>
> I think she's getting fatter
>
> And fatter
>
> And fatter
>
> And fatter
>
> Pop!

Wendy and Caroline make copies of their "How to Have Fun with Blubber" list and distribute them to the class. When the girls force Linda to eat a chocolate-covered ant, she throws up all over the desk and floor. Linda never returns to class that day; Mr. Nichols, the school principal, comes instead. Wendy is a master liar and proceeds with an explanation that is so smooth that she shocks her classmates. Jill is beginning to feel uncomfortable with Wendy's bossy ways and cruel behavior, but, like most 10-year-olds, she isn't strong enough to stand on her own and take up for Linda.

Things begin to change for Jill when her family goes to Warren Winkler's bar mitzvah and she is seated at the same table with Linda Fischer. To Jill's surprise, she and Linda are asked to light the thirteenth candle on Warren's birthday cake. But, there is still some doubt in Jill's mind about being friends with Linda. There is the question about who squealed on Jill and Tracy for putting eggs in Mr. Machinist's mailbox on Halloween. Wendy tries to convince the girls that Blubber is surely the squealer, but Tracy, who isn't in the class with the other girls, is doubtful. At Jill's suggestion, the class puts Linda on trial, but Wendy quickly takes over, bullying her way through the entire event. She doesn't want to give Blubber a lawyer and insists that everything be done her way. At this point, Jill finally takes charge and tells Wendy, "I'm sick of you bossing everyone around. If Blubber doesn't get a lawyer then Blubber doesn't get a trial."

It's difficult not to be scared of Wendy, but Jill bravely enters the classroom the next morning only to discover that Wendy has adopted Linda as her friend and the entire class has turned on Jill. Of course, Jill still has Tracy Wu, her oldest and best friend, but there is no one in her class with whom she can eat lunch except for the class loner, Rochelle. As lonely as Jill feels, she does realize "You sometimes have to make the first move or else you might wind up like Linda—letting other people decide what's going to happen to you."

Blume's keen ear for dialogue, her understanding of kids and their need to be part of a group, and her desire to raise questions related to the cruelties of life make *Blubber* one of her most significant novels for middle-grade readers. She hits the issues hard, never sugar coating the conflict, and makes her characters so real that readers are convinced that she is seated in their classroom. *Blubber* is a tough novel, but it is an important book to use with students to help them understand hurt, cruelty, and downright meanness. How does it feel when loyalties change and you suddenly find yourself on the other side of the fence? Jill Brenner finds out and suffers in the process. But, she also changes on the inside, an important lesson for Jill, and for her readers.

SETTING THE SCENE

Ask students to discuss the familiar saying, "Sticks and stones may hurt my bones, but words will never hurt me." Then, engage them in a discussion about how words really can hurt.

DISCUSSION

- Some people think that kids shouldn't read *Blubber* because of the way the kids treat each other and the language that the characters use. Discuss whether you have ever witnessed a student bullying another student. Why do people become bullies? What is the best way to deal with a bully? How does reading about a "real" situation prepare you for dealing with a similar situation? Why are some adults afraid of discussing "real" issues with kids?

- Why is Linda such an easy target for bullies like Wendy? What problems might Wendy have in her life that make her such a bully?

- Discuss the qualities of a true friend. Describe Jill and Tracy's friendship. How do you know that their friendship will be lasting?

- Read the passage on page 95 where Jill talks about cursing, and discuss whether her observation about why people use bad language is true. What is an appropriate response to someone who uses bad language to your face?

- Why is Wendy's Halloween costume an appropriate one for her? What does it say about her personality?

- How do you think Linda Fischer feels when the kids in her class are mean to her? How would you feel if you were in Linda's shoes?

- Brainstorm adjectives that best describe Wendy. How do you know that she is the real "troublemaker" in her class? Jill says, "It's important to be Wendy's friend." Why do the other kids follow Wendy's lead? Why do you think Linda is willing to be Wendy's partner on the class trip?

- Jill feels that she will win the prize for the most original costume at her school's Halloween Parade. She says that the prize doesn't matter to her, but she likes the idea of winning. Why is winning so important to Jill? Discuss her reaction when Fred Yarmouth wins for his fried egg costume. How is the desire to win the same as the desire to be popular?

- Discuss the meaning of the term "sour grapes." How does Jill display sour grapes when Kenny comes home and announces that he has won the contest in his class for the most original costume?

- Jill's mom says, "A person who can laugh at herself will be respected." Debate whether this statement is true. Why is it so difficult to laugh at yourself?

- Mrs. Minish asks Jill to redo her math work sheet because she did the equations backward. Jill feels that this is unfair because she got the answers right. Why is setting up a problem properly as important as getting the right answer? Discuss whether Jill is being rude to Mrs. Minish when she asks, "Isn't there more than one way to think?" Locate other incidents in the novel where Jill appears rude.

- Jill seems to have a warped sense of what is right and wrong. Why does she think that smashing someone's pumpkins on Halloween isn't right, but putting rotten eggs in a person's mailbox is okay?

- Jill tells Tracy that she's not hanging around with Wendy anymore because "she acts like she owns the whole world." Tracy replies, "I've always known that." Discuss why Tracy sees through Wendy long before Jill does.

- When Jill is so distraught because no one likes her anymore, she dissolves into tears at the dinner table. Her mom asks if she wants to talk about what's bothering her. Why is talking about pain and hurt feelings important?

- At the beginning of the novel, Jill says that Tracy Wu, her best friend, tells her that she is really tough on people. At the end of the novel, Mrs. Brenner tells Jill, "You can be a pretty tough character sometimes." Discuss how Jill changes from the beginning of the novel to the end.

- Discuss the phrase "Turnabout is fair play." Debate whether Jill gets what she deserves at the end of the novel when Wendy blocks her from using the toilet and calls her "Baby Brenner."

- One of the challenges to *Blubber* concerns the perception that in the book, "bad is never punished. Good never comes to the fore. Evil is triumphant." Discuss whether evil really is triumphant in the book. The book is about Jill, not Wendy or Linda. What lessons does Jill learn about evil? How is Jill triumphant?

ACTIVITIES

- Define harassment. Discuss the relationship between harassment and bullying. Most schools have a student handbook that details school rules. Look at your school's handbook. Is there a rule about harassment? Based on your school's rule, discuss whether Linda could have accused her classmates of harassment. Then, role-play a scene in which Linda discusses her problem with the school principal. Why should teachers, principals, and parents be informed of such behavior?

- Jill dresses as a flenser, a person who removes blubber from a whale, for the costume contest at her school's Halloween Parade. Think of an unusual career or job and decide the type of dress that best represents that career. Have a class Career Costume Day where everyone comes to school in appropriate dress for a specific career.

- There are references to health issues like smoking, sun bathing, and obesity mentioned in *Blubber*. With a group of classmates, prepare an oral presentation to the class that discusses the health hazards related to one of these issues and what medical science is doing to make the public aware of these hazards.

- Halloween has become dangerous in many cities across the nation. With classmates, share things that your city, community, neighborhood, and church or synagogue are doing to help kids stay safe at Halloween. Plan a Halloween party for younger kids. Begin by brainstorming an appropriate theme. Games, refreshments, costumes, decorations, and invitations should reflect the theme chosen by the class.

- Linda decides to go on a diet and eats celery, yellow cheese, and saltines for lunch. Discuss whether this is a healthy diet. Invite the school nurse or a nutritionist to speak to your class about healthy eating. Then, study the food groups and the recommended daily calorie intake for a 10-year-old. Make a diet and exercise plan for Linda to follow.

- Wendy and Caroline compile a list called "How to Have Fun with Blubber." There are six mean things on the list. Brainstorm at least six ways to be nice to Linda.

- *Blubber* is written in first person from Jill Brenner's point of view. Select a scene from the novel where the kids are especially mean to Linda, and rewrite the scene from Linda's point of view. How does the tone of the scene change? Discuss whether changing the point of view makes the reader more sympathetic to Blubber.

- Judy Blume, the author of *Blubber,* compiled a book titled *Letters to Judy: What Your Kids Wish They Could Tell You.* In this book, Blume shares many letters that she has received from young readers asking for help. Read the following letter that Judy Blume received and write a response to the letter.

> Dear Judy,
>
> I am in fourth grade. I wanted to tell you that I have a million problems. My friends always gang up on me. They kicked me out of the play one week before the actual play. They put a new girl in my place. They're always doing things like that to me. They pass dirty notes about me to me! They call me bad names and they don't know what they mean. They don't know the difference between stupid and dumb. They don't even know what a bitch is. All of them tell lies. Sometimes my friends come back and want to be friends again, but then, the next day, they just gang up on me like before. What should I do?

- Ask your parents to share stories about bullies when they were in school. If your parents agree, relate these stories in class. What do these stories reveal about the nature of bullying?
- Jill and Tracy never know who squealed on them for putting rotten eggs in Mr. Machinist's mailbox. When Wendy blames Blubber, Jill suggests that they have a trial. With your classmates, conduct two mock trials, one for Linda and the other for Wendy. Appoint student lawyers and a judge. Who is guilty based on evidence uncovered in the trial?
- Sometimes, teachers are unaware of situations involving bullies in the classroom and on school buses. Discuss whether Mrs. Minish is aware of the ways her students bully one another. Role-play a scene in which Mrs. Minish talks to Jill and the other girls in the class about their behavior.

FICTION CONNECTIONS

Brown, Susan M. *You're Dead, David Borelli.* 1995. 155p. Atheneum.

AGES 9–12   When David's mother dies and his father is jailed for embezzling funds from his company, David is sent to a foster home and, for the first time in his life, encounters schoolyard bullies and uncaring teachers.

Byars, Betsy. *The 18th Emergency.* 1973. 126p. Viking.

AGES 9–12   Ezzie knows all the answers to most any emergency except what to do if Marv Hammerman, the class bully, comes after him.

Cox, Judy. *Mean, Mean Maureen Green.* Illustrated by Cynthia Fisher. 2000. 80p. Holiday House.

AGES 8–10   When Maureen, the third-grade bully, is assigned to Lilley's school bus, Lilley must confront her fears and, in the process, learns that Maureen's words are tougher than her actions.

Dadey, Debbie. *King of the Kooties.* 1999. 112p. Walker.

AGES 9–12   At the beginning of the school year, fourth-grader Donald is the target of Louisa, the class bully, and Nate, his best friend, must help him learn to defend himself.

Fine, Anne. *The Tulip Touch.* 1997. 160p. Little, Brown.

AGES 9–12   Natalie becomes friends with Tulip, a girl who tells lies, talks back to teachers, and plays evil tricks on others. When Natalie tries to escape from Tulip, she fears what Tulip may do to her.

Fletcher, Ralph. *Spider Boy.* 1997. 183p. Clarion.

AGES 9–12   Newcomer Bobby Ballenger, an expert on spiders, comes face-to-face with the class bully and finally begins to find his own place.

Hahn, Mary Downing. *Stepping on the Cracks.* 1991. 216p. Clarion.

AGES 9–12   Sixth-graders Margaret and Elizabeth encounter Gordy, the feared school bully, and learn something about his home life that helps them understand his mean ways.

Hiser, Constance. *Ghosts in Fourth Grade.* Illustrated by Pat MacDonald. 1992. 68p. Holiday House.

AGES 8–11   James and his friends plot to scare Mean Mitchell, the class bully, by turning the old Hathaway house into a haunted house on Halloween night.

Korman, Gordon. *The 6th Grade Nickname Game.* Illustrated by Mark Buehner. 2000. 160p. Hyperion.

AGES 9–12   Eleven-year-old Jeff and Wiley pride themselves in their ability to pick the perfect nickname for everyone in their class, but when they attempt to nickname Cassandra, a new classmate, things get testy, and they almost ruin their friendship.

Laird, Elizabeth. *Secret Friends*. 1999. 80p. Putnam.

AGES 9–12   Being friends with Rafaella, a girl with large ears and a funny name and who is a social outcast, could ruin Lucy's chances of becoming one of the "in" crowd at school. When she calls Rafaella "Earwig" in front of their classmates, the other kids think it is funny and begin teasing Rafaella; Lucy soon regrets what she has done, but not before a tragedy strikes.

McNamee, Graham. *Nothing Wrong with a Three-Legged Dog*. 2000. 128p. Delacorte.

AGES 9–12   Lynda is called "Zebra" because her mother is black and her father is white. Keath, her best friend, comes face-to-face with Toothpick, a bully, who has it in for him because Keath is white in a black school.

Meade, Alice. *Junebug and the Reverend*. 1998. 192p. Farrar, Straus & Giroux.

AGES 9–12   Junebug moves to a new neighborhood when his mother becomes caretaker of an apartment building for senior citizens. There he struggles to cope with his new life, including bullying classmates and the responsibility of walking a retired minister every day. A sequel to *Junebug*.

Moss, Marissa. *Amelia Takes Command*. 1999. 40p. Pleasant Co.

AGES 9–12   Hilary, the class bully, is a constant pest to Amelia, but when Amelia goes to Space Camp, she takes command of a mock space shuttle mission and, in the process, learns to deal with Hilary. Readers will also enjoy *Amelia's Notebook* (1995), *Amelia Writes Again* (1996), and *Amelia Hits the Road* (1997).

Mulford, Philippa Green. *Emily Smiley and the Mean Queen* (Emily Smiley, No. 1). 1998. 128p. Tor Books

AGES 8–11   Nine-year-old Emily is dealing with a new stepmother and three stepbrothers, and to make matters worse, she is the target of the fourth-grade bully, Missy Atkins.

Sachar, Louis. *The Boy Who Lost His Face*. 1997. 198p. Random House.

AGES 9–12   After taunting an elderly woman, Danny Ballinger loses his popularity at school when he receives a curse, and he quickly learns the price of popularity.

Sachs, Marilyn. *Veronica Ganz.* 1995. 134p. Puffin.

AGES 9–12   No one messes with Veronica Ganz, the biggest girl in the class, until Peter Wedemeyer proves that he is not frightened of her by demonstrating his many sneaky ways of getting to her.

Schenker, Dona. *The Secret Circle.* 1998. 160p. Knopf.

AGES 10–13   Jamie, a new student at an exclusive private school, learns a hard lesson about the power of cliques and the importance of following one's own conscience.

Sheldon, Dyan. *My Brother Is a Superhero.* Illustrated by Derek Brazell. 1996. 128p. Candlewick.

AGES 9–12   Nine-year-old Adam and his friend Midge have problems with a group of school bullies, but instead of asking his brother for help, Adam devises a plan to stand up to them.

Shreve, Susan Richards. *Joshua T. Bates in Trouble Again.* Illustrated by Roberta Smith. 1997. 96p. Knopf.

AGES 9–12   After repeating third grade, Joshua is moved to fourth grade midyear and must find a way to deal with Tommy Wilhelm, his sworn enemy and the class leader. A sequel to *The Flunking of Joshua T. Bates* (1984) and *Joshua T. Bates Takes Charge* (1993).

Sonenklar, Carol. *Mighty Boy.* 1999. 128p. Orchard Books.

AGES 9–12   In this funny novel, Howard, a new kid and small for his age, is bullied by a classmate. Through his obsession with *Mighty Boy,* a television show, Howard finds a way to wipe out his tormentor.

Spinelli, Jerry. *Wringer.* 1999. 240p. HarperCollins.

AGES 9–12   Palmer is 9 years old and is dreading the day when he turns 10 because he is expected to become a wringer, a boy who strangles wounded pigeons during the town's annual pigeon shoot.

Venokur, Ross. *The Amazing Frecktacle.* 1998. 128p. Delacorte.

AGES 9–12   Nicholas Bells is the target for teases and taunts because of his bright red hair, unusual right eye, and abundant freckles. Tired of the cruel nicknames, he seeks an instant cure for his freckles.

Yep, Laurence. *Cockroach Cooties*. 2000. 208p. Hyperion.

AGES 9–12   Teddy and Bobby, two brothers first introduced in *Later, Gator* (1997), are often at odds with one another, but they quickly learn the meaning of "brotherly love" when Bobby is attacked by a bully at school and Teddy comes to his rescue.

STRATEGY 4

The Goats

Farrar, Straus & Giroux   1987   183 pages

BROCK COLE

AGES 12–UP

*I'm socially retarded for my age, she said with a certain
dignity. Yeah. Me too.*

—Laura and Howie, age 13, in *The Goats*

The need to belong is a driving need among young adolescents. Their relationship with their family and how they view themselves greatly affect who
they are and their ability to interact and form relationships with others.
Young teens who are "different" often suffer ridicule from their peers and
have a difficult time making friends. This is the underlying conflict of
Brock Cole's *The Goats*. Howie is 13 years old and labeled a social outcast.
His parents are archaeologists who spend the summers in exotic places
excavating pottery and other things that are clues to ancient civilizations.
This particular summer, they decide that Howie, an only child, needs to be
around boys his own age. Instead of taking him with them to Turkey, they

---

This strategy has been adapted from an article first published in *Book Links*, September 1997.

send him to camp. Howie doesn't adjust well to camp, and the other campers tease and taunt him, naming him the camp "goat."

At a neighboring camp for girls, 13-year-old Laura is considered a "loner." The only child of a business woman whose main interest is climbing the corporate ladder, Laura has spent most of her young life alone or surrounded by adults. When she is sent to camp, where she is expected to relate to girls her own age, she becomes acutely aware that she is "socially retarded." She, too, is named the camp "goat."

The tradition at the two camps is to take the "goats" by boat at night to an island in the middle of the lake, strip them of their clothing, and leave them there alone. The "goats" are normally retrieved at daybreak, but this time things are different. While Howie and Laura are considered "misfits," the other campers have no clue that these two are bright, courageous young people who will find their own way to fight back. Laura is the first left on the island. When Howie arrives, Laura's quiet whimpering noises lead him to her. He finds her wrapped in an old blanket sitting on a dilapidated tent platform. Frightened and humiliated, Laura listens as Howie unfolds his plan for their escape. He instructs Laura, who cannot swim, to hold on to a log while he pulls the log and swims to shore in the opposite direction of the camps. The two aren't quite sure what will happen when they get to shore; but, the one thing they are sure of is that both camps will realize that their cruel idea of a joke isn't so funny after all.

Howie's and Laura's simple plan turns into quite an adventure. They break in to a summer cottage where they find clothing that is much too big, and food that is old and stale. After resting awhile, they make their way up the beach, searching for ways to get food and clothes that fit so that they won't be so conspicuous. Realizing that the camps have probably reported them missing, the two are constantly on the lookout for the police. When, at one point, they think that they have been spotted, they jump on a school bus with a group of teenagers going to a camp for underprivileged kids. These streetwise campers from the city smuggle Howie and Laura into their cabins for the night and the next morning, send the two runaways off after filling their empty stomachs with a good breakfast. Their next stop is the Starlight Motel. Laura finds a way to get a room for the night, and Howie, who is suffering from a cold, is skeptical but agreeable. They take showers, enjoy a good night's sleep, and awake to face a questioning housekeeper. This time, they take off down the highway and steal a deputy sheriff's truck. They make their way to some nearby woods where they begin thinking seriously about their situation.

Along the way, never revealing her location or the fact that she has left camp, Laura has called her mother asking for permission to come home and to bring Howie with her. Too busy to be bothered by her daughter, Laura's mother lectures her about staying at camp. Finally, the camp notifies Mrs. Golden that her daughter is missing. When she learns of the camps' cruel treatment of Laura and Howie, Mrs. Golden threatens the owners with a lawsuit. Howie's parents cannot be reached. Laura and Howie realize that it is inevitable that they give up. They agree to meet Laura's mother, who is waiting for them on the edge of the woods.

For a long time, Howie and Laura didn't even know each other's name, but their shared plight was enough to help them build a strong friendship. They know that they will have to face the camp directors and the police. Howie knows that he will eventually face a telephone conversation with his parents. He has no idea what they will say to him or how they will react to the situation. Will they fault him? Will they blame the camp?

Regardless of what happens now, Laura and Howie know that from this time forward, things will be different. They each have a *friend*, a very good *friend*. And, most importantly, they have learned much about themselves and their ability to survive. Whether their peers ever accept them is unknown. It no longer matters to the "goats." "They can look at each other now and smile."

DISCUSSION

- Describe Laura's relationship with her mother. What do you think Mrs. Golden's secretary thinks of their relationship? How do you think Laura's experience at summer camp will change their relationship?

- In reference to Parents' Weekend, Mrs. Golden says to Laura, "Well, I'm coming. I mean, if you're having problems, I've got to, haven't I?" Why is Mrs. Golden's reason for coming to Parents' Weekend the wrong reason? How do you think Mrs. Golden contributes to making Laura a "misfit"?

- Howie "knew he was afraid to leave her alone, but more important, it wouldn't be good enough. He wanted them both to disappear. To disappear completely." Explain why Howie wants them to completely disappear. Does he want this for them, or does he simply want to retaliate against the camp?

- Howie and Laura are considered "misfits." How do you treat people who are "misfits" or "outcasts" in your classroom? What things can you do to make them feel more accepted?

- The camp director tries to pass off the incident as a "joke." Why would he see humor in humiliating a camper? Why is cruelty to others never a joke?

- Throughout the novel, Laura and Howie keep a record of the things they have taken so they can pay the people back. How can they possibly repay people they don't even know? Do you think they really intend to repay the people, or does the thought of it simply ease their consciences?

- Sometimes writers use open endings in their novels to give readers the opportunity to make up their own mind about what happens. What do you think happens when Laura and Howie find Mrs. Golden? Do they remain at camp for the rest of the summer? If so, how do the other campers treat them?

- At West Point Military Academy, the cadet who ranks last in the class is called a "goat." How is this person's situation similar to Laura and Howie's situation? It is customary for the cadet that is the "goat" of the class to receive cheers and applause at graduation. Why do you think this happens? Why is it unlikely that Howie and Laura will receive this type of tribute when they return to camp?

- Howie and Laura are well into their adventure before they learn each other's name. Why do you think they don't introduce themselves by name when they first meet?

- Find evidence in the novel that Howie and Laura are extremely bright individuals. Why do you suppose they never stop to think about the dangers involved in running away? Discuss the many dangers they might have encountered.

- Discuss whether Howie and Laura's summer camp experience might help them better relate to their classmates in the fall.

- *The Goats* has been challenged and actually removed from some school libraries because "it contains a passage describing a naked girl," and because it is "morally offensive and inappropriate for middle school students." What might be considered "morally offensive" about this book? Sometimes, books that make us a little uncomfortable are the ones that make us think about the important issues in life. Discuss how *The Goats* might be considered such a novel. What is life-changing about this book?

ACTIVITIES

- Write a letter that Howie might write to his parents explaining his experience at camp.

- Laura tells Howie that the campers will probably come back to the island to get them. Dramatize the scene that isn't in the book when the other campers come back and find that Howie and Laura have disappeared.

- Look up the word *goat* in the dictionary. What is the U.S. slang usage of the word? Considering this meaning, why are Howie and Laura named the "goats?"

- Read *One Fat Summer* by Robert Lipsyte. Compare and contrast Bobby's relationship with Joanie to the relationship that develops between Howie and Laura.

- Pardoe calls Howie and Laura "Bonnie & Clyde." Go to the library and find information about the real Bonnie and Clyde. Why do you think Pardoe gives Howie and Laura these nicknames?

- Pardoe says that "it isn't smart to go running around in the woods. People see you. They wonder what you're doing. . . It's better in the city. Nobody cares." Read *Slake's Limbo* by Felice Holman. Compare and contrast Slake's experience running away in the city with Howie and Laura's experience in the woods. Is Pardoe's theory right?

- Make a list of all the things that Howie and Laura take during their adventure. Calculate how much money they owe.

- The novel is written in third person. How would the story change if it were written in first person? Pick a favorite scene in the novel, and rewrite it in first person from either Howie's or Laura's point of view.

- Brock Cole uses similes to create certain images (for example, "His beautiful plan was coming apart like wet paper."). Find other examples of similes in the novel.

- Pretend that you are a television reporter. Write a news story about Howie and Laura's disappearance. Then, tape an on-the-spot news story when they are found. Include an interview with Howie and Laura, the camp directors, other campers, and Mrs. Golden. Stage a debate about hazing or camp and school traditions that place others in humiliating and dangerous situations.

FICTION CONNECTIONS

Belton, Sandra. *Ernestine and Amanda: Summer Camp, Ready or Not!* 1997. 168p. Simon & Schuster.

AGES 11–14 Growing up in the 1950s, Ernestine and Amanda are constant rivals until they attend different summer camps and discover much about themselves and the importance of friendship.

Blacker, Terence. *Homebird.* 1993. 139p. Bradbury.

AGES 11–14 Thirteen-year-old Nicky Morrison is a misfit and cannot adjust to the British boarding school that he attends. He runs away and takes up life in an abandoned building in London, and tries to come to terms with his family problems.

Brown, Alan, and Grant Forsberg. *Lost Boys Never Die.* 1989. 116p. Delacorte.

AGES 10–13 Eleven-year-old Lewis Dee is scheduled to go to speech camp while his parents explore the Arctic Circle, but instead returns home, where he lives for eight weeks, encountering the neighborhood bully and some unlikely friends who change his life.

Feuer, Elizabeth. *Lost Summer.* 1995. 185p. Farrar, Straus & Giroux.

AGES 10–12 Twelve-year-old Lydie Ayles faces some painful truths about her relationship with family and friends when she goes away to summer camp and encounters a misfit, Karen.

Holman, Felice. *Slake's Limbo.* 1974. 117p. Scribner.

AGES 10–13 Because 13-year-old Aremis Slake is a loner and little for his age, he lives in fear of the neighborhood bullies and takes refuge in the New York subway.

Kroll, Steven. *Breaking Camp.* 1985. 169p. Macmillan.

AGES 12–UP Ted Jenner, a high school junior, learns much about courage when he discovers that the pranks at Camp Cherokee are really attacks on "weaker" boys.

Lipsyte, Robert. *One Fat Summer.* 1977. 152p. HarperCollins.

AGES 12–UP Overweight Bobby Marks has never known how to stand up for himself until the summer of his fourteenth year when he finds a job cutting grass for Dr. Kahn, a mean and greedy man, and faces the local bully, Willie Rumson. *Summer Rules* and *The Summerboy* continue Bobby's story through his adolescence and reveal his inner growth as an individual.

Lynch, Chris. *Slot Machine.* 1995. 241p. HarperCollins.

AGES 12–UP   Though Elvin isn't athletic and is somewhat of a misfit, he is hauled off to a summer retreat with other freshman boys entering the Christian Brothers Academy where coaches will "slot" them into specific sports. A coming-of-age novel about what it's like to be nonathletic surrounded by athletic peers.

Mango, Karin N. *Portrait of Miranda.* 1993. 232p. HarperCollins.

AGES 12–UP   Her classmates don't accept Miranda, a junior in a private high school, because she appears overly dramatic and somewhat obnoxious. When she finds out the truth about a family mystery involving her grandmother, she begins her journey toward understanding and believing in herself.

Milton, Hilary. *Nowhere to Run.* 1978. 153p. Watts.

AGES 12–UP   When a summer visit with their father and stepmother doesn't work out, Wayne and Linda Pollard, feeling unwanted and very vulnerable, decide to run away in search of a place to call their own.

Sachs, Marilyn. *At the Sound of the Beep.* 1990. 154p. Dutton.

AGES 12–UP   Upset by their parents' divorce, Matthew and Mathilda Green run away to live in Golden Gate Park and find themselves in the middle of a mystery involving the homeless people in the park.

Savage, Deborah. *Under a Different Sky.* 1997. 276p. Houghton Mifflin.

AGES 12–UP   More than anything, 18-year-old Ben wants to ride his horse, Galaxy, in the Olympics. His chances are dim until he meets an extremely rebellious rich girl from the exclusive private boarding school that borders his family's farm. Torn between reality and dreams, both teenagers embark on an inner journey that helps them understand themselves and, eventually, each other.

Sinykin, Sheri Cooper. *The Buddy Trap.* 1991. 129p. Atheneum.

AGES 12–UP   Misfit Cam Whitney would rather be playing his flute than facing the antagonism and hazing delivered by his tentmates at Camp Rainbow Lake.

Spinelli, Jerry. *Stargirl.* 2000. 176p. Knopf.

> AGES 12–UP   Stargirl has been home-schooled until tenth grade when
> she enters Mica High. For a while, she is a mystique to the students,
> but her weird ways and her unwillingness to follow the crowd soon
> cause her to be shunned by everyone except Leo Borlock, who falls in
> love with her.

Townsend, John Rowe. *Dan Alone.* 1983. 214p. HarperCollins.

> AGES 12–UP   Eleven-year-old Dan Lunn longs for a life in a happy fam-
> ily, but runs away to avoid going to an orphanage. He meets Olive and
> Leo, who introduce him to a new family, a group of thieves who teach
> him to beg.

Summer Trilogy

One Fat Summer

Harper & Row   1977   153 pages

Summer Rules

Harper & Row   1981   150 pages

The Summerboy

Harper & Row   1982   150 pages

ROBERT LIPSYTE

AGES 12–UP

*I always hated summertime. When people take off their clothes.
In wintertime you can hide yourself. . . But in the summertime
they can see your thick legs and your wobbly backside and your big
belly and your soft arms. And they laugh.*

—Bobby Marks, age 14, in *One Fat Summer*

In *One Fat Summer*, 14-year-old Bobby Marks is doomed to spend the summer with his family at Rumson Lake, a community where many New
Yorkers go to escape the heat and the fast-paced life of the city. To overweight Bobby, the lake means swimming. Swimming means taking off your
clothes. Taking off your clothes means revealing your fat body to the local
Rumson boys so they can call you names like "Crisco Kid."

This strategy was adapted from an article first published in *Book Links*, September 1998.

Bobby's only plan for the summer is to complete a school project with Joanie, his best friend and supporter. To his surprise, Joanie mysteriously returns to the city, leaving him with nothing to do but to sit around and feel sorry for himself. Mr. Marks tries to help by suggesting that Bobby busy himself by working as a counselor in a day camp or as a mother's helper. Bobby hates his father's suggestions and secretly takes a job as a yard boy for Dr. Kahn. The summer is looking better for Bobby, especially when he realizes that physical labor is causing him to lose weight. Then Willie Rumson, a jobless town bum, decides that he wants Bobby's job. When Bobby refuses to relinquish the job, Willie threatens to gun him down. At this point, Bobby's newly discovered confidence is put to the test. With only a rusty Cub Scout knife in his pocket for defense, Bobby takes on Willie in an underwater fight. Willie, who is not used to losing, is surprised when Bobby, an excellent swimmer, defeats him without ever using the knife.

Bobby Marks is 16 years old and thinner in *Summer Rules*. He is tougher and more self-confident and ready to do "real man's" work by helping Jim Smith, a local landscape gardener. However, Bobby's father, a city slicker who considers the locals at Rumson Lake "trash," has made other plans for him. He thinks being a camp counselor is a more appropriate job for Bobby. Michelle, Bobby's older sister, is already on the staff of the Happy Valley Day Camp and reluctantly agrees to ask Moe Bell, the camp director, to hire her brother. Bobby's challenge begins when he takes over the "Atom Smashers," a group of 10-year-olds with the worst reputation in camp. Harley Bell, Moe Bell's nephew and the terror of the camp, is in Bobby's group. Harley is so emotionally disturbed that he consumes all of Bobby's time, taking Bobby's attention away from the other campers.

Being a man with an imagination, Bobby devises a plan for Harley. If the plan works, the other campers will be free to enjoy camp, and Bobby will be free to spend more time with Sheila, his summer heartthrob. Things are going well, and everyone is in high spirits until tragedy strikes the camp. The casino goes up in flames, and Bobby is faced with a "real man's" job of telling the truth and saving Willie Rumson, his old enemy, from being accused of a crime he did not do.

In *The Summerboy*, the last book in the trilogy, Bobby is 18 years old and finally lands a "real man's" job. Having just completed his freshman year in college, he returns to Rumson Lake for the summer with the idea of working at Lenape Laundry with the tough guys. This time, his parents have less influence on his decision. Mr. and Mrs. Marks have remained in the city for the summer, and his sister is spending the summer in Europe.

Now that he has the house to himself, Bobby feels a surge of independence and boldly approaches Roger Sinclair, the new owner of the laundry, for a job. Mr. Sinclair is doubtful that the local workers will accept a summerboy but he decides to take a risk and tells Bobby, "The job is yours if you can hack it." Bobby intends to prove that he is more than a soft college boy looking for a summer taste of real man's work. He is eager to sweat and labor with the locals, but meets head-on with rejection and discovers working conditions that threaten the safety of the laundry employees.

After a week on the job, Bobby learns that Roger Sinclair has no interest in the laundry and even less interest in making things better for his discontented workers. When Sinclair asks Bobby to spy on the volatile employees, Bobby calls it snooping and eventually turns his support to the workers. A series of events causes Bobby to stand up to Sinclair and demand that the employees be heard. Bobby's notion that hard labor makes a man proves to be partially true. His active involvement in fighting Sinclair on behalf of the workers and helping his friend, Joanie, out of a difficult situation help him discover the true qualities of manhood.

This autobiographical trilogy is appropriately told in first person. Bobby's constant wisecracks and his skill for making puns make his toughest situations laughable. Lipsyte is a master storyteller with an amazing understanding of adolescence and a special knack for humor. Young adults most often label him "a writer who makes real life seem funny."

■ *ONE FAT SUMMER*

SETTING THE SCENE

Robert Lipsyte's three books about Bobby Marks are considered coming-of-age novels. Discuss the term *coming-of-age*. At what age do most young adults begin their journey to adulthood? List some of the physical and emotional characteristics that identify coming-of-age.

DISCUSSION

- The novel begins the summer of Bobby's fourteenth year. How does Bobby describe himself? Why does he hate summertime?

- How does Bobby get the courage to call Dr. Kahn about the lawn job? Why does he choose to keep his summer job a secret from his family? At what point does Bobby discover that his mother knows about his job?

- Discuss why Bobby is always making up stories about heroes.

- Bobby says that he and Joanie are good pretenders. Do you think Bobby really is a good pretender? Why?

- "Rule number one: never let people know they can get to you or they'll never stop trying." Find incidents in the novel where Bobby lets people get to him.

- Describe Willie Rumson. Why is he so angry? Why is Bobby a victim of Willie's anger?

- Bobby's father says, "A man has to do something with his life." What do you think Mr. Marks wants Bobby to do with his life?

- What does Joanie mean when she asks Bobby, "Are you a man or a rug?" Find incidents where Bobby is a "rug." Find incidents where he is a "man."

- Dr. Kahn advertises the lawn job for one dollar per hour, but offers Bobby only 75 cents an hour. Why does Bobby accept the job? Why do you think Dr. Kahn keeps Bobby on if he is so dissatisfied with Bobby's work? What makes Bobby continue to work when he takes so much verbal abuse from Dr. Kahn?

- Michelle says to Bobby, "I guess you will be a writer when you grow up. . . .You're such a liar already." Why would Michelle think that lying is a qualification for becoming a writer?

- Why do you think Pete jumps Willie when the problem between Bobby and Willie has been solved? Why do Bobby and Michelle hate Pete for his actions? What does Bobby mean when he says that "Pete didn't know any more about being a man than I did."

- In reference to his summer job, Bobby says, "I probably should have told Mom the truth. She would have helped me convince Dad. But then she would have interfered, driven over to look at Dr. Kahn's lawn, maybe even talked to Dr. Kahn. I wanted this to be all mine." Why is it important for Bobby to have a job that is all his? Think about experiences or situations that you have wished to keep secret. Why was this important to you? How may this desire for privacy reflect your need for independence?

- When Bobby's mother doesn't notice his weight loss, he says, "She didn't really look at me. Nobody really looks at people in their own house."

Do you think your family members really look at each other? What things would you like for your family to notice about you? How can you be a better observer?

- *One Fat Summer* has been challenged because it is "sexually explicit and full of violence." Locate passages in the book that cause challengers to accuse the novel of being violent and sexually explicit. How are these passages necessary to show Bobby's journey toward becoming a man?

ACTIVITIES

- Write a journal entry that Bobby might have written the day he got the job at Dr. Kahn's. Write another entry that he might have written on the day that he told Dr. Kahn that he underpaid him.
- Pretend that Bobby visits a support group for overweight teens. Prepare and deliver a speech that Bobby might give.
- Design a "split-screen" collage that reveals the changes that occur within Bobby from the beginning of the novel to the end.
- Act out the scene in chapter 19 in which Bobby has the encounter with Willie.
- Bobby is always making up stories about heroes. Write a story making Bobby the hero.

■ *SUMMER RULES*

DISCUSSION

- Why does Bobby's father want him to work at Happy Valley Day Camp? Why does Bobby think Happy Valley should be called "Pathetic Molehill"?
- "Taking care of spoiled brats was no real man's job." How would Bobby describe a "real man's" job? Why do you think having a "real man's" job is so important to Bobby?
- Bobby says about Joanie, "I started to miss her. Then I remembered she was dating college men these days." Why do you think this would make a difference in their relationship?

- Bobby's father asks, "Aren't you sorry now you put up such a fuss about going to Happy Valley?" What does Bobby mean when he says, "It was a rhetorical question, no answer required"?

- How do the Rumsons and Smiths view the summer people? How does Bobby's father view summer renters? Discuss how the renters are different from the people who own summer homes.

- Describe Harley's behavior. Why does Harley have behavior problems? How does Bobby's plan for Harley help the other campers?

- "Like all true bullies, he [Harley] picked his victims with care." What kinds of people do bullies pick? Discuss whether Harley is really a bully.

- When Bobby gets drunk at the counselors' party and Jim Smith finds him and takes him home, Bobby's father is angry because he thinks that Bobby has been out with Jim. Discuss why Michelle doesn't tell her father the truth about where Bobby has been.

- "I was jealous. Joanie and Stewart could talk poetry and make literary jokes with each other. . . .Sheila didn't know who I was any more than I knew who she was." Describe Bobby and Sheila's relationship. At what point does Bobby start losing interest in Sheila? What type of girl is Bobby really looking for?

- Bobby tries to have a discussion with his father about lying, but Mr. Marks tries to get off the subject. Why do you think it is difficult for Mr. Marks to discuss lying?

- Why do you think that Bobby goes to the police and tells them that Willie Rumson didn't burn the casino?

- Moe Bell says that "winning isn't everything." Do you think society puts too much emphasis on winning in sports and other competitions? What are some things that could be more important than winning? Describe something that you would enjoy doing if less emphasis were put on winning.

ACTIVITIES

- In old magazines, find pictures that best resemble the following characters: Bobby, Michelle, Jerry, Moe Bell, Sheila, and Harley. Using the pictures, make a camp memory book. Label each picture with an appropriate quote from the novel.

- "Imagination, I thought, where would a writer be without it." Reread the section of the novel in which Bobby uses his imagination to get Harley to come down from the roof of the casino. Embellishing the story that Bobby tells, write a horror story about a buzzard attack on Harley.

- Pretend that you are a radio or television reporter. Tape an on-the-spot news story about the fire at Happy Valley. Include an interview with Moe Bell and Jerry Silver.

- Play the music from *The King and I,* and identify Jerry's song. Write a paper contrasting the lyrics of the song with growing up.

■ *THE SUMMERBOY*

DISCUSSION

- Describe the Lenape Laundry. Why does Bobby want to work at the laundry? What specific job does he want to do? Why do you think Roger Sinclair hires Bobby?

- "I'd cut grass and I'd been a day-camp counselor, and last summer I was a lifeguard at Spiro's Lakeside, but I had never had a real job before." Why doesn't Bobby consider any of his previous jobs "real jobs"?

- Roger Sinclair fires Bobby after the accident with the laundry truck. Why does he then hire him back?

- Discuss why Bobby decides to stay at the laundry after such a hard first week on the job. Why does Jim Smith try to get Bobby to quit?

- Describe Roger Sinclair. What is his attitude toward the laundry? What are his feelings toward the laundry workers? Why is he afraid of Bobby?

- What does Mr. Sinclair mean when he says, "Marks, old chap, you've got to learn that the hero walks through the crowd without becoming one of the crowd"?

- Bobby says that he and Joanie "had been friends since they were three years old, and we'd helped each other through plenty of rough times." What are some of the rough times that Bobby and Joanie have shared?

- When Bobby quit the laundry after the first week on the job, he says, "I left behind a few people whose respect I would have liked to earn." Who do you think those people are? Why?

- "She [Joanie's mother] never asked me a direct question. She's afraid I might tell her the truth and then she'll have to deal with it." Why is it so hard for some people to deal with the truth? What are some things that you think your parents have a difficult time facing? How can dealing directly with the truth encourage better communication between you and your parents?

- Bobby says, "I'd made a commitment to her [Joanie] as a friend, and I couldn't let her get caught because of me." What does it mean to make a commitment to someone? Name situations in which keeping a commitment to a friend may be a wrong decision. Discuss the qualities of "true friendship."

ACTIVITIES

- Bobby Marks reads and studies good literature. He mentions Ernest Hemingway, John Steinbeck, and J. D. Salinger. Select one of these writers and prepare a brief report about his contribution to American literature.

- Bobby gives his parents quick character sketches of Axel, Lolly, and Ace. Select one of these characters or pick any other character from the laundry and write a brief character sketch.

- Read several movie reviews from a local or a regional newspaper or both. Note the style of writing and the kinds of things reviewers notice. View Bobby's favorite movie, Shane. Then, write a review of the movie for the Rumson Lake Gazette.

- Research the origin and purposes of unions. Discuss the advantages and disadvantages of union involvement in such businesses as the Lenape Laundry. Then, write a letter to Roger Sinclair stating your position on unionization.

LINKING THE NOVELS

- Willie Rumson in One Fat Summer and Harley in Summer Rules may be considered bullies. Considering the difference in their ages, how are their actions similar? How are the reasons for their behavior different?

- Dr. Kahn, Moe Bell, and Roger Sinclair all take advantage of Bobby. Compare and contrast the actions of each of these men. How does the experience of working with each of these men contribute to Bobby's development as a man?

- Bobby has a poor self-image in *One Fat Summer*. As he gets older, he develops a more positive sense of self. Write a paper contrasting Bobby's self-image at age 14 with his self-image at age 18.

- Bobby says that Joanie likes the poetry of Emily Dickinson. Find a Dickinson poem that Bobby might give to Joanie in *One Fat Summer*, and a poem that he might give to her in *The Summerboy*. How do these poetry choices reflect changes in Bobby and Joanie?

- Ask your parents or other adults to tell you about the television program *I've Got a Secret*. Stage the show, choosing the secrets from the three novels.

- Prejudice comes in many forms. Identify specific expressions of prejudice in each of the novels. What causes people to develop prejudices? What is the difference between prejudice and bigotry? Why is it important to develop tolerance and an understanding of others?

FICTION CONNECTIONS

Carkeet, David. *Quiver River*. 1991. 236p. HarperCollins.

AGES 12–UP   During the summer following their junior year in high school, Ricky and his friend Nate take a job at a summer resort in the Sierra mountains, where they begin their journey into manhood. Sequel to *The Silent Treatment*.

Cohen, Barbara. *Fat Jack*. 1980. 182p. Atheneum.

AGES 12–UP   Participating in a senior class play helps two teenage outcasts begin to understand betrayal and the true meaning of friendship.

Crutcher, Chris. *Athletic Shorts: Six Short Stories*. 1991. 154p. Greenwillow.

AGES 12–UP   Characters from many of Crutcher's novels appear in these short stories that explore the inner lives of young adolescent males.

Crutcher, Chris. *Staying Fat for Sarah Byrnes*. 1993. 216p. Greenwillow.

AGES 12–UP   Contemporary issues, such as abortion, organized religion, and suicide, are among the topics that a senior class discusses in an effort to support a friend who is crying for help.

Friel, Maeve. *Charlie's Story*. 1997. 144p. Peachtree.

AGES 12–UP   Growing up in Dublin, Ireland, Charlotte Collins (Charlie) wants to be accepted by her peers, but instead is tormented by the in-crowd at school.

Holland, Isabelle. *The House in the Woods*. 1991. 194p. Little, Brown.

AGES 12–UP   Bridget wants the love of her adoptive father, and she longs to be thinner and more attractive. When she decides to give up her fantasies and face the real world, she becomes involved in a mystery that changes her outlook on life.

Holt, Kimberly Willi. *When Zachary Beaver Came to Town*. 1999. 227p. Holt.

AGES 10–UP   Zachary Beaver, the fattest boy in the world, comes to Antler, Texas, in the summer of 1971. At first, people tease him and call him unkind words, but when Toby Wilson and his friend Cal get to know Zachary, they find out the true meaning of friendship.

Janeczko, Paul B. *Preposterous: Poems of Youth*. 1991. 134p. Orchard Books.

AGES 12–UP   This collection of poetry about growing up treats the problems and concerns of adolescents in both a serious and humorous manner. More than half of the poems are told from the male point of view.

Joosse, Barbara M. *The Pitiful Life of Simon Schultz*. 1991. 137p. HarperCollins.

AGES 12–UP   The only way that eighth-grader Simon Schultz can deal with the trauma caused by his overbearing mother is to record his private thoughts in a journal.

Kerr, M. E. *Dinky Hocker Shoots Smack!* 1972. 198p. Harper & Row.

AGES 12–UP   Overweight Dinky Hocker doesn't appear bothered by her mother's encounter-groups-at-home, or by her boyfriend's attempt to get her to join Weight Watchers, but when she finally has enough, she finds a unique way to get the attention she needs.

Marino, Jan. *Like Some Kind of Hero.* 1992. 216p. Little, Brown.

AGES 12–UP Ted wants to be considered a hero and be noticed by the girls, so he takes a summer job as a lifeguard, where he quickly learns what being a true hero really means.

Newman, Leslea. *Fat Chance.* 1994. 214p. Putnam.

AGES 12–UP Like most 13-year-old girls, Judi wants to be thin and popular with the boys. Instead, she is fat and struggles with a poor self-concept. Through daily diary entries, she records her most personal thoughts regarding her dreams

Silvey, Anita, ed. *Help Wanted: Short Stories about Young People Working.* 1997. 174p. Little, Brown.

AGES 11–UP Twelve short stories by such writers as Gary Soto, Norma Fox Mazer, Ray Bradbury, Tim Wynne-Jones, and Michael Dorris explore the working world of young adults.

Skinner, David. *The Wrecker.* 1995. 106p. Simon & Schuster.

AGES 12–UP Michael, a new kid at school, is enlisted by Theo, the boy genius, to plot a scheme that will make everyone's life better by wrecking the eighth-grade class bully.

Strasser, Todd. *How I Changed My Life.* 1995. 186p. Simon & Schuster.

AGES 12–UP The search for a new identity is the theme of this novel about an overweight girl and a former high school football player.

Zindel, Paul. *The Undertaker's Gone Bananas.* 1978. 239p. Harper & Row.

AGES 12–UP In this zany novel, two teenagers are convinced that a neighbor, an undertaker, has killed his wife.

STRATEGY 6

Roll of Thunder, Hear My Cry

Dial Books   1976   276 pages

MILDRED D. TAYLOR

AGES 10–14

Children, I come back today
To tell You a story of the long dark way
That I had to climb, that I had to know
In order that the race might live and grow.

—From "The Negro Mother"
in Langston Hughes's *Selected Poems*

The Great Depression was an economic nightmare for most American families, but blacks living in the rural South suffered hardships far greater than those caused by the depressed economy. In the 1930s, the South was a white society. White landowners controlled local businesses and government, schools and churches were segregated, and white children were taught to feel superior to blacks. A few black families were fortunate enough

---

This strategy is adapted from an article originally published in *Book Links,* January 1995.

to own their own land, but most sharecropped on land owned by ᵥ
do whites. Black men, women, and children worked side by side
fields, toiling long hours for very little money. Many blacks were foɪ
supplement their meager wages by working as domestics in the hoɪ
whites. Almost daily, blacks came face-to-face with cruel acts of ɾ
There were no civil rights laws to protect them, so they were often cl
out of their earnings, mistreated on the job, and humiliated on the streets
of small towns and cities. But, in spite of their daily encounters with racial
bigotry, most black families survived, because of their strong sense of family and deep commitment to one another.

In *Roll of Thunder, Hear My Cry*, the 1977 Newbery Medal winner for
middle and junior high school readers, Mildred D. Taylor tells of one black
family's struggle against poverty and of its determination to keep its most
cherished possession—four hundred acres of rich Mississippi land. Three
generations of Logans live under one roof on the land that Grandpa Logan
purchased in 1887. Now, in the middle of the Great Depression, the
Logans are in trouble. For three years, their cotton crop hasn't brought in
enough income to pay the expenses of the farm, and Harlan Granger, the
white man whose family once owned the Logan land, is set on getting the
land back and rebuilding the original Granger plantation.

Told from the point of view of nine-year-old Cassie, the Logans' story
begins in October, when the crops are in and the black children start their
school year. David Logan, Cassie's father, is away in Louisiana, laying track
for the railroad to earn extra cash to pay the farm debts. Big Ma Logan, now
in her 60s, is left in charge of running the household, while Mary Logan,
Cassie's mother, teaches school and manages the farm. Stacey, Cassie,
Christopher John, and Little Man, the four Logan children, are too young to
appreciate the value of the land and their father's intense effort to save it. But,
they *are* old enough to realize the racial discrimination that envelops their life.
When Stacey and Cassie go with Big Ma to Strawberry, a nearby small
town, to sell milk and eggs, Cassie is the victim of several acts of racism. In
Mr. Barnett's store, she is forced to wait until the white customers have been
helped, and Lillian Jean Simms, a white girl, blocks Cassie's path on the
sidewalk and demands that Cassie apologize for trying to pass her. Then, as
the Logan children make their daily walk to the Great Faith Elementary and
Secondary School, they are splattered with mud by the school bus that takes
the white children to the Jefferson Davis County School.

Just as the Logan children are struggling to understand the injustice of
the school system and the daily torture they receive from the white
schoolchildren, more serious acts of racism erupt in their lives. The threat

of the Night Riders is looming, and Mary Logan is fired from her teaching position for lodging a protest against the secondhand textbooks. Then, the Wallaces, owners of a local store, badly burn some of the sharecroppers. When Papa comes home to help organize a boycott of the Wallaces' store, he is shot in the leg and loses his job with the railroad. At this point, the threat of losing the Logan land brings Uncle Hammer, Papa's brother, home from Chicago. Hammer Logan isn't a wealthy man, but he does own a car, which he willingly sells to get money to pay off the land debts. Once the farm debts are settled, Papa is faced with a greater challenge. T.J. Avery, Stacey's smooth-talking friend, takes up with the white Simms boys and robs Mr. Barnett's store. Mr. Barnett is murdered, and T.J. is blamed. The Wallaces, the Simmses, and a posse of white men form a lynching party and go after T.J. The Logans, however, are certain that T.J. didn't kill Mr. Barnett, and believe he is being accused because he is black. In an effort to see that T.J. receives a trial, Papa distracts the mob by setting fire to his own cotton field. T.J. is rescued, turned over to the sheriff, and taken to jail.

The economic and societal pressures of the times are against the Logans, but they never lose their self-respect in spite of the brutal humiliation they experience. Readers will admire the Logans' love for one another, their strong sense of values, and their unrelenting effort to save their land. Above all, they will respect David Logan's willingness to make personal sacrifices for the sake of justice. The story can also serve to stimulate discussion about the problem of continuing intolerance and what might be done. Taylor continues the Logans' story and their fight against racial discrimination in other novels listed in the bibliography.

SETTING THE SCENE

Read aloud "The Negro Mother" by Langston Hughes. Discuss the living conditions for African Americans in the South in the 1930s. Then analyze Hughes's poem. What does Hughes mean when he makes reference to "the long dark way"? Why does he think it is important for people to understand the past?

DISCUSSION

- The Logan children are made to wear their Sunday clothes on the first day of school. Why does Mrs. Logan feel that the beginning of school is so special?

- Cite evidence that the Avery family is poorer than the Logan family.

- Why is Stacey so upset about having his mother as his teacher? T.J. says, "Jus' think of the advantage you've got." Why does T.J. see Stacey's situation as an advantage? Why does having his mother as a teacher turn out to be a disadvantage for Stacey?

- The white children begin their school year in August, but the black children don't start school until October. Why is their school year different?

- The bus driver likes to entertain his white passengers by splattering mud on the black children as they walk the dirt roads to school. What do they finally do to get back at the bus driver?

- Why do the other teachers at the black school consider Mary Logan a "disruptive maverick"?

- What does Miss Crocker mean when she tells Mary Logan that she is "biting the hand that feeds her"?

- How is Jeremy Simms different from other members of his family? Why does he befriend the Logan children?

- T.J. is a smooth talker. How does he manipulate Stacey? What does Stacey learn from his unfortunate dealings with T.J.?

- Why does Mary Logan organize a boycott of the Wallaces' store? Why is boycotting difficult for people like Mr. Turner?

- Describe Cassie's day when Big Ma finally invites her to go into town. Why does Big Ma make Cassie apologize to Lillian Jean for an incident that isn't Cassie's fault? How does Cassie eventually get back at Lillian Jean?

- "Baby, we have no choice of what color we're born or who our parents are or whether we're rich or poor. What we do have is some choice over what we make of our lives once we're here." What does Cassie make of her life?

- *Roll of Thunder, Hear My Cry* has been challenged in schools across the country because of racial bias. Discuss the difference between racial bias and racial discrimination. How does the racial discrimination in the novel reflect the time and place of the story? Why is it important to understand rather than deny that discrimination exists?

ACTIVITIES

- The white children attend the Jefferson Davis County School, but the black children attend the Great Faith Elementary and Secondary School.

Go to the library and locate information about Jefferson Davis. Why would a black school never be named for him? Identify black leaders who were prominent before the Great Depression. Then, rename the black school in honor of one of them. Share and justify your choice.

- Cassie's mother grew up on the Delta, but the Logan land is in Spokane County. Draw an outline of the state of Mississippi and label Spokane County and the area of the state known as the Delta. Why is it called the Delta? Calculate the approximate number of miles from the Delta to Spokane County.

- The Logans took their cotton to be ginned at the Granger place. Research the ginning process. Who invented the cotton gin? Write an essay about how the cotton gin changed cotton farming.

- The Logans and their black neighbors are threatened by the Night Riders. Who were the Night Riders? What organization did they represent?

- The 1964 Civil Rights Act was the strongest civil rights bill in U.S. history. Research the provisions of this act. Make a chart listing the many ways this act changed the lives of minorities in the United States.

- What is the significance of the 1954 *Brown vs. Board of Education* decision? Draw a political cartoon about this event.

- Langston Hughes was a famous black poet. Locate and read some of his poems. For each member of the Logan family, select a poem that you would like to dedicate. Then, write an appropriate dedication at the top of each poem and make an anthology. Illustrate the cover.

- Find out the difference between civil liberties and civil rights. Explain how the Logans's civil liberties and rights are violated. Bring a newspaper to class and locate an article that states or implies that someone's civil rights or liberties have been violated.

- Locate the poem "Freedom Train" by Langston Hughes. In a small group, prepare a choral reading of the poem.

- The author's father was a storyteller. Ask someone in your family to relate a story to you. Prepare the story for retelling, and share it with the class.

- Taylor uses similes to create certain images (for example, "the narrow, sun-splotched road wound like a lacy red serpent"). Find other examples of similes.

OTHER BOOKS BY MILDRED TAYLOR

The Friendship. 1987. 56p. Dial.

AGES 9–11   When a young black boy saves the life of a white boy, a special friendship is developed. Now, as adults, their relationship is affected by acts of racism.

Let the Circle Be Unbroken. 1981. 394p. Dial.

AGES 10–14   In this sequel to *Roll of Thunder, Hear My Cry*, it is now 1935. The Logans and their black neighbors continue to be victims of racial antagonism and hatred, especially when T.J. Avery is tried for murder by an all-white jury.

Mississippi Bridge. 1990. 64p. Dial.

AGES 9–11   Jeremy Simms tells this story of the day his black friends are forced to get off the bus to make room for late-arriving white passengers. When the bus goes over the railing of a bridge, it is a young black man who helps rescue the people.

The Road to Memphis. 1990. 288p. Dial.

AGES 12–UP   Cassie, now a senior in high school, with dreams of attending college and law school, finds that no amount of education prepares her for the racial tension that erupts in Jackson, Mississippi.

Song of the Trees. 1975. 56p. Dial.

AGES 9–11   In the first of the Logan stories, the family is desperately trying to raise enough money to pay the taxes on its beloved land. While David Logan is away laying tracks for the railroad, his mother is cheated by a white man selling timber from the Logan land.

The Well: David's Story. 1995. 96p. Dial.

AGES 9–11   Set in 1910, when David Logan is a boy, this latest Logan story tells about a Mississippi drought that leaves most farm families without water. When the Logans offer to share their well with white as well as black families, two of the Simms boys contaminate the water with dead animals.

FICTION CONNECTIONS

Armstrong, William H. *Sounder.* Illustrated by James Barkley. 1969. 116p. HarperCollins.

AGES 10-UP   The boy's father is a sharecropper, but times are hard. When the father steals some meat to feed his hungry family, he is arrested and taken far away to prison, leaving the boy to be the man of the family.

Carbone, Elisa. *Storm Warriors.* 2001. 137p. Knopf.

AGES 10-UP   Nathan Williams, an African American boy who lives on the North Carolina coast, dreams of becoming a surfman, but his father sees his ambition as "pipe dreams" because the position of surfman is a "white man's" job.

Curtis, Christopher Paul. *Bud, Not Buddy.* 1999. 245p. Delacorte.

AGES 10-14   During the Great Depression in Flint, Michigan, 10-year-old Bud, an orphan, sets out on a tough journey in search of the man he believes is his father.

Gaines, Ernest J. *The Autobiography of Miss Jane Pittman.* 1971. 256p. Bantam.

AGES 12-UP   This fictionalized account for older readers tells how Pittman, a black woman born into slavery, organizes and participates in a freedom demonstration a century later.

Herlihy, Dirlie. *Ludie's Song.* 1988. 224p. Dial.

AGES 12-UP   A 13-year-old white girl learns some harsh realities about racial discrimination when she befriends a black girl who has been disfigured by a suspicious fire, in this novel set in rural 1950s Georgia.

Krisher, Trudy. *Spite Fences.* 1994. 283p. Delacorte.

AGES 12-UP   In a small town in Georgia in the 1960s, Maggie Pugh, the adolescent narrator, teaches an old black man how to read, and because of her relationship with him, becomes involved in the civil rights movement.

Meyer, Carolyn. *White Lilacs.* 1993. 242p. Gulliver Books.

AGES 9-12   Based on a true story, this novel, set in Texas in 1921, traces the troubles of a black community when the whites try to take over their land to make a park.

Moore, Yvette. *Freedom Songs.* 1991. 176p. Orchard.

AGES 12–UP After 14-year-old Sheryl travels south in 1963 and experiences segregation, she returns to Brooklyn and organizes a fund-raising event to support the freedom riders.

Nelson, Vaunda Micheaux. *Mayfield Crossing.* Illustrated by Leonard Jenkins. 1993. 96p. Putnam.

AGES 9–11 In 1960, the black kids from Mayfield Crossing are being transported to Parkview Elementary, where they encounter racism. Baseball finally unites the races.

Rabe, Berniece. *Hiding Mr. McMulty.* 1997. 256p. Harcourt.

AGES 12–UP Eleven-year-old Rass Whitley sets out to help Mr. McMulty, an elderly black man, who has been cheated by his landlord during the Great Depression in Missouri.

Springer, Nancy. *They're All Named Wildfire.* 1989. 112p. Atheneum.

AGES 10–14 Springer's story, set in rural Pennsylvania, finds Jenny, a white girl, learning hard lessons about racial bigotry when she makes friends with Shanterey, a black girl who moves into the duplex next door.

Staples, Suzanne Fisher. *Dangerous Skies.* 1996. 232p. Farrar, Straus & Giroux.

AGES 12–UP A black girl in a small town in Virginia is falsely accused of murder and her best friend, a white boy, experiences the harsh realities of racism even within his own family.

Walter, Mildred Pitts. *The Girl on the Outside.* 1982. 150p. Lothrop.

AGES 12–UP Sophie, a white student, and Eva, a black student, are the main characters in this fictional account of the integration of Central High School in Little Rock, Arkansas, in 1957. Also note the author's *Because We Are* (Lothrop, 1983).

Wilkinson, Brenda. *Not Separate, Not Equal.* 1989. 152p. HarperCollins.

AGES 12–UP In 1965, 17-year-old Malene Freeman, the daughter of a poor sharecropper, is orphaned, and her adoptive parents insist that she be one of the first black students to integrate the white high school in a small Georgia town.

NONFICTION CONNECTIONS

Beals, Melba Patillo. *Warriors Don't Cry: A Searing Memoir of the Battle to Integrate Little Rock's Central High.* 1995. 220p. Pocket/Archway.

AGES 12–UP   The dramatic story of Melba Patillo Beals's part in the dramatic battle to integrate Little Rock's Central High School in 1957 can be contrasted with Robert Coles and George Ford's picture book *The Story of Ruby Bridges* (Scholastic, 1995).

Bullard, Sara. *Free at Last: A History of the Civil Rights Movement and Those Who Died in the Struggle.* 1994. 112p. Oxford.

AGES 12–UP   The history of the civil rights movement is presented in a journalistic style in one concise volume that includes a time line of events and profiles of 40 people who died during that time. Contemporary black-and-white photos enhance the text.

Duncan, Alice Faye. *The National Civil Rights Museum Celebrates Everyday People.* Photographs by J. Gerard Smith. 1995. 64p. BridgeWater Books.

AGES 10–UP   This photo-documentary tour of the National Civil Rights Museum pays tribute to the men, women, and children who changed our nation's history through their involvement in the civil rights movement.

Fireside, Harvey, and Sarah Betsy Fuller. *Brown vs. Board of Education: Equal Schooling for All.* 1994. 128p. Enslow.

AGES 10–UP   The authors discuss the ideas and arguments surrounding this 1954 landmark Supreme Court case giving equal education to all.

Haskins, James. *The Scottsboro Boys.* 1994. 118p. Holt.

AGES 12–UP   Haskins documents the 1931 landmark case of nine black youths who were charged with assault against two white women in Alabama.

Hughes, Langston. *Selected Poems.* 1959. 297p. Knopf.

AGES 12–UP   These poems celebrate the accomplishments of black people and reflect the musical rhythms of jazz, the blues, and spirituals for which Hughes is so noted. Also see Hughes's *The Dream Keeper and Other Poems* (Knopf, 1935).

Levine, Ellen. *Freedom's Children: Young Civil Rights Activists Tell Their Own Stories.* 1993. 224p. Putnam.

AGES 12–UP   Thirty southern blacks who were children and teenagers in the 1950s and 1960s share their firsthand experiences with the civil rights movement.

McKissack, Patricia, and Frederick McKissack. *A Long Hard Journey: The Story of the Pullman Porter.* 1989. 144p. Walker.

AGES 10–14   Chronicles the history of the Brotherhood of Sleeping Car Porters, the first African American union, focusing on specific events during the Great Depression years.

Myers, Walter Dean. *Now Is Your Time! The African-American Struggle for Freedom.* 1991. 320p. HarperCollins.

AGES 12–UP   A comprehensive history of the African American quest for freedom, beginning in 1619 and continuing through the modern civil rights movement.

Rochelle, Belinda. *Witnesses to Freedom: Young People Who Fought for Civil Rights.* 1993. 97p. Lodestar.

AGES 10–UP   The stories of young people who witnessed and were involved in such events as the Montgomery bus boycott, *Brown vs. Board of Education*, and various sit-ins during the civil rights movement.

Tillage, Leon Walter. *Leon's Story.* Illustrated by Susan L. Roth. 1997. 107p. Farrar, Straus & Giroux.

AGES 9–11   Leon tells about the years that his father was a share-cropper and the family lived in fear of the Ku Klux Klan.

The Watsons Go to Birmingham—1963

Delacorte   1995   210 pages

CHRISTOPHER PAUL CURTIS

AGES 12–UP

I ain't never heard of no sickness that makes you kill little girls just because you don't want them in your school. I don't think they're sick at all, I think they just let hate eat them up and turn them into monsters.

> —Byron Watson, age 13, in
> *The Watsons Go to Birmingham–1963*

The Watsons Go to Birmingham–1963 is often presented as a work of fiction about the civil rights movement. Though the novel is set during the 1960s when race riots were occurring in the South, the story is really about family relationships, friendship, and love. The civil rights movement is significant to the story, but what the "Weird Watsons" learn about one another on their journey from Flint, Michigan, to Alabama is what brings the initial conflict to a comfortable and even tender resolution. Ten-year-old Kenny is bullied by his older brother Byron, an "official juvenile delinquent." Kenny, an excellent student, is quiet and serious. He is attentive to his younger sister, Joetta, and is extremely sensitive to the needs and problems of his friends. Thirteen-year-old Byron has already failed two grades and seems to be making no progress toward improvement. Instead of devoting time to schoolwork, Byron spends his free time finding out how much trouble he can create at home and at school. Kenny seems to be the best target for Byron and his gang until Rufus Fry moves to the Watsons' neighborhood. Like Kenny, who is burdened with being smart and having a lazy eye, Rufus has two things against him. Rufus is from the South and speaks with a southern drawl, and his clothes are tattered and torn. Kenny and Rufus become soul mates until one day Kenny forgets what real friendship is about and joins in when the kids on the school bus laugh at the clothes Rufus is wearing. When Kenny finally gets the nerve to tell his mother how he has hurt Rufus, Mrs. Watson walks Kenny to the Frys' house and helps Kenny make amends.

Mrs. Watson doesn't seem to have the same skill in dealing with Byron. In fact, she is so disgusted with his behavior that she and Mr. Watson decide to deliver Byron to Grandma Sands in Birmingham, Alabama. The deal is that Byron will stay in Birmingham for the summer and if there is no change in his behavior, he will extend his stay through the following school year. Though the Watsons have heard about the race riots in Alabama, Grandma Sands assures them that things are quiet and safe where she lives.

Two things happen in Birmingham that change the purpose of the Watsons' trip. Kenny, ignoring a no-swimming sign, almost drowns and is rescued by Byron. Grateful that Byron pulls him from the "Wool Pooh," Kenny is amazed when he sees his brother shake and break into sobs, an uncharacteristic behavior for Byron. Then, all the news stories about the political and social problems in the South are made real when a church in Grandma Sands's neighborhood is bombed. Thinking that Joetta is a casualty at the church, the frightened Watsons run from the house in search of the little girl. Though Joetta is safe, Mr. and Mrs. Watson take their three children and leave that night, swearing to tell no one what they witnessed in Birmingham.

Kenny is the person who suffers the most from the memories of the trip. He becomes solemn and silent, and shows no interest in reuniting with his friends. When he withdraws into his own world and begins hiding behind the couch, Byron sleeps on the couch so that Kenny won't be alone with his thoughts. Finally, in a memorable scene, Byron takes on the role of a caring big brother. As Kenny sits in the bathroom sobbing and replaying the scene of the bombing, Byron assures him, "There ain't nothing wrong with being sad or scared about that. I'm sad about it too. I got real scared too."

SETTING THE SCENE

Use the library or appropriate sites on the Internet to find out events related to the civil rights movement in 1963. Make a time line of the most significant events. Discuss these events, and why they were important to the social issues of the time.

DISCUSSION

- Who is the main character of the novel? Discuss the conflict of the story. How do the near-tragic incidents contribute to the resolution of the conflict?

- Describe the Watson family. Discuss Kenny's relationship with Byron. Byron's feelings toward Kenny change at the end of the novel. Discuss whether Byron will continue to support Kenny and be a better brother to him.

- Humor is sometimes expressed in what characters say. Other times, it is expressed in what they do. Discuss the humor in the novel. How does Christopher Paul Curtis create humor?

- The kids make fun of Kenny because he is smart. How do Kenny's teachers make things worse for him? Discuss the reasons why being smart should be "cool." How are smart kids recognized in school? Discuss whether kids like Byron would benefit from some type of incentive program where rewards are given for trying to do better in school.

- The bus driver tells Rufus, "Don't you pay no mind to them little fools, they ain't happy lest they draggin' someone down." Why do people feel the need to "drag others down"? What can you do in school to make those who are different feel welcome? What does *intolerant* mean? How is intolerance related to bullying, prejudice, and overt acts of racism?

- What does Mrs. Watson mean when she says that in Birmingham, "Things aren't perfect, but people are more honest about the way they feel"? Discuss the various types of racism. How is silent or "covert" racism a more serious type of racism?

- Discuss what Mrs. Watson does to prepare her children for the trip to Birmingham. What is the thing that she cannot prepare them for?

- Mrs. Watson doesn't want to tell anyone what her family saw in Birmingham. Why is such silence dangerous to our society? What do you think Kenny Watson will tell his children about his trip to Birmingham? Why is it important to read books about bitter periods in our history?

ACTIVITIES

- Kenny tells Joetta that he is going to write his own comic book and call it "Lipless Wonder." Select a humorous scene from the novel, and write and illustrate a short comic book based on the scene.

- The opening scene of the novel is extremely funny. On one of the coldest days in Flint, Byron gets his lips stuck to the outside mirror of the car. Find out the lowest temperature in Flint, Michigan, in 1963. Then, find the coldest day in Birmingham, Alabama. Compare and contrast the climate of the two cities.

- The Watsons go to Birmingham in the summer of 1963 and witness the bombing of an African American church. Locate articles about the bombing of the Sixteenth Avenue Baptist Church in Birmingham on September 15, 1963. Compare and contrast this bombing to the bombing of African American churches in the United States in the late 1990s. What conclusions can be drawn about racism in our country today?

- Read *Burning Up* by Caroline Cooney (Delacorte, 1999). Compare and contrast the way Kenny deals with the bombing of the church in Birmingham to the way Macey Clare deals with the bombing of the inner-city church near her small town in Connecticut. How does such racism make Macey work harder to uncover the haunting truth behind a fire in her town in the 1960s?

- Find out about the students who integrated Central High School in Little Rock, Arkansas, in 1957. Write a letter that Kenny Watson might write to these students after his trip to Birmingham in 1963.

- In the Epilogue to *The Watsons Go to Birmingham–1963*, Christopher Paul Curtis says, "It is almost impossible to imagine the courage of the first African American children who walked into segregated schools or the strength of the parents who permitted them to face the hatred and violence that awaited them. They did it in the name of the movement, in the quest for freedom." Prepare a dramatic tribute to these children. Include poetry, songs, excerpts from civil rights speeches, and original compositions.

- Visit the Web site of the Birmingham Civil Rights Institute (http: //bcri.bham.al.us). What is the significance of the street address of the Civil Rights Institute? There are permanent exhibits in seven galleries at the Institute. Describe these exhibits. What is the purpose of the traveling exhibit? What type of information might one find on a virtual field trip to the Institute?

- Use reference books to identify specific locations of significant civil rights events (for example, Montgomery, Alabama; Memphis, Tennessee; Washington, D.C.). Use a road atlas of the United States and plan a trip for tourists who are interested in the history of the civil rights movement. Prepare a pamphlet that highlights special attractions.

FICTION CONNECTIONS

Cooney, Caroline. *Burning Up.* 1999. 240p. Delacorte.

AGES 12–UP   Fifteen-year-old Macey Clare conducts a local history project and learns the real meaning of racism when she uncovers the truth behind a 38-year-old fire that threatened the life of an innocent black man in her small Connecticut town.

Grove, Vicki. *The Starplace.* 1999. 208p. Putnam.

AGES 11–13   In Oklahoma in the 1960s, Celeste, the first black girl to attend Quiver Junior High, is cut from the chorus just before a very important competition. The story reveals the harsh realities of racism and its effects on the school and community.

Hewett, Lorri. *Lives of Our Own.* 1998. 214p. Dutton.

AGES 12–15   Shawna Riley moves with her father to his hometown in Georgia where she encounters unexpected racism and uncovers a secret from her father's past that links her to one of the popular white girls at school.

Krisher, Trudy. *Spite Fences.* 1994. 283p. Delacorte.

AGES 12–UP   In a small town in Georgia in the 1960s, Maggie Pugh, the adolescent narrator, teaches an old black man how to read, and because of her relationship with him, becomes involved in the civil rights movement.

Lynch, Chris. *Gold Dust.* 2000. 192p. HarperCollins.

AGES 10–UP Napoleon Charlie Ellis, a kid from Dominica, and Richard Riley Moncrief are promising baseball stars on the Little League field until racism threatens their friendship.

Marino, Jan. *The Day That Elvis Came to Town.* 1991. 204p. Little, Brown.

AGES 11–13 Wanda's life is dull until a glamorous singer arrives at her mother's boarding house and promises that her show business connections can arrange a meeting between Wanda and Elvis Presley. Wanda never meets Elvis, but she does come face-to-face with racism in her small southern town in the 1960s.

Moore, Yvette. *Freedom Songs.* 1991. 176p. Orchard.

AGES 10–UP After 14-year-old Sheryl travels south in 1963 and experiences segregation, she returns to Brooklyn and organizes a fund-raising event to support the freedom riders.

Nelson, Vaunda Micheaux. *Beyond Mayfield.* 1999. 144p. Putnam.

AGES 10–12 Meg's quiet life in Mayfield is threatened when she is the victim of racial discrimination at school, and she becomes acutely aware of the harsh treatment of civil rights workers in the South in the 1960s.

Nelson, Vaunda Micheaux. *Mayfield Crossing.* Illustrated by Leonard Jenkins. 1993. 96p. Putnam.

AGES 9–11 In 1960, the black kids from Mayfield Crossing are being transported to Parkview Elementary, where they encounter racism. Baseball finally unites the races.

Wilkinson, Brenda. *Not Separate, Not Equal.* 1989. 152p. HarperCollins.

AGES 12–UP In 1965, 17-year-old Malene Freeman, the daughter of a poor sharecropper, is orphaned, and her adoptive parents insist that she be one of the first black students to integrate the white high school in a small Georgia town.

Woodson, Jacqueline. *The House You Pass on the Way.* 1997. 99p. Delacorte.

AGES 11–14 At 14 years old, Staggerlee Canan, the middle child of a mixed-race family, struggles to understand the racist world around her, and embarks on a journey that gives meaning to the work of her grandparents, activists who died in a civil rights demonstration in Alabama in 1969.

Young, Ronder Thomas. *Learning by Heart.* 1993. 172p. Houghton Mifflin.

AGES 9–12   Ten-year-old Rachel moves with her family to a small southern town in the 1960s and learns lessons about friendship, racism, and prejudice from a black housekeeper.

NONFICTION CONNECTIONS

Beals, Melba Patillo. *Warriors Don't Cry: A Searing Memoir of the Battle to Integrate Little Rock's Central High.* 1995. 220p. Pocket/Archway.

AGES 13–UP   The story of Melba Patillo Beals's part in the dramatic battle to integrate Little Rock's Central High School in 1957. Can be contrasted with Robert Coles and George Ford's picture book *The Story of Ruby Bridges* (Scholastic).

Bell, Janet Cheatham, and Lucille Usher Freeman. *Stretch Your Wings: Famous Black Quotations for Teens.* 1999. 176p. Little, Brown.

AGES 12–UP   A book of quotations from famous African Americans like Martin Luther King Jr., Marian Wright Edelman, and Denzel Washington dealing with topics and themes about racism, civil rights, family, love, and setting goals.

Bridges, Ruby. *Through My Eyes.* 1999. 64p. Scholastic.

AGES 8–12   Ruby Bridges tells her story as a 6-year-old in 1960 walking through a group of segregationists to be the first African American child to attend an all-white elementary school.

Bullard, Sara. *Free at Last: A History of the Civil Rights Movement and Those Who Died in the Struggle.* 1994. 112p. Oxford.

AGES 11–15   This history of the civil rights movement, presented in a journalistic styl   ⌐ludes a time line of events and profiles of 40 people who died during that time. Contemporary black-and-white photos enhance the text.

Duncan, Alice Faye. *The National Civil Rights Museum Celebrates Everyday People.* Photographs by J. Gerard Smith. 1995. 64p. BridgeWater Books.

AGES 10–UP   This photo-documentary tour of the National Civil Rights Museum pays tribute to the men, women, and children who changed our nation's history through their involvement in the civil rights movement.

Haskins, Jim. *Separate but Not Equal: The Dream and the Struggle.* 1998. 192p. Scholastic.

AGES 8–12   A history of the ongoing struggle of African Americans for equal education.

Haskins, James. *The March on Washington.* 1993. 144p. HarperCollins.

AGES 11–UP   Black-and-white photographs document this account of the 1963 March on Washington.

King, Casey, and Linda Barrett Osborne. *Oh Freedom! Kids Talk about the Civil Rights Movement with the People Who Made It Happen.* Illustrated by Joe Brooks. 1997. 32p. Knopf.

AGES 10–14   The text of this historical account of the civil rights movement of the 1950s and 1960s is taken from actual interviews that fourth-graders conducted with everyday people who were directly involved with the struggle for civil rights.

Kronenwetter, Michael. *America in the 1960s.* 1998. 112p. Lucent.

AGES 11–15   The entire decade of the turbulent 1960s, including the assassinations of J.F.K. and Martin Luther King Jr., the Cold War, and the civil rights movement, is discussed and documented with black-and-white archival photographs.

Levine, Ellen. *Freedom's Children: Young Civil Rights Activists Tell Their Own Stories.* 1993. 224p. Putnam.

AGES 10–UP   Thirty southern African Americans who were children and teenagers in the 1950s and 1960s share their firsthand experiences with the civil rights movement.

McKissack, Patricia, and Frederick McKissack. *The Civil Rights Movement in America from 1865 to the Present.* 1991. 351p. Children's Press.

AGES 12–UP   A history of the civil rights movement, beginning with Reconstruction and ending with a discussion of race-related problems among other minorities.

Meltzer, Milton. *There Comes a Time: The Struggle for Civil Rights.* 2001. 192p. Random House.

AGES 12–UP   Beginning with the landing of the first slave ships, this book outlines African Americans' struggle for "life, liberty, and the pursuit of happiness," and discusses the important events of the civil rights movement of the 1960s.

Myers, Walter Dean. *Now Is Your Time! The African-American Struggle for Freedom.* 1991. 320p. HarperCollins.

AGES 11–UP   A comprehensive history of the African American quest for freedom, beginning in 1619 and continuing through the modern civil rights movement.

Powledge, Fred. *We Shall Overcome: Heroes of the Civil Rights Movement.* 1993. 214p. Scribner.

AGES 12–UP   The history of slavery in the United States is discussed, but the focus is on 10 individuals who participated in the civil rights movement.

Rochelle, Belinda. *Witnesses to Freedom: Young People Who Fought for Civil Rights.* 1993. 97p. Lodestar.

AGES 12–UP   *Brown vs. Board of Education,* the Montgomery bus boycott, and other significant civil rights events are discussed, focusing on the young people who participated.

Webb, Sheyann. *Selma, Lord, Selma: Girlhood Memories of the Civil-Rights Days.* 1980. 146p. University of Alabama Press.

AGES 12–UP   Two girls, Sheyann and Rachel, tell their stories about their participation in the civil rights demonstrations in Selma, Alabama, in 1965.

STRATEGY 8

Bridge to Terabithia

Crowell   1977   128 pages

KATHERINE PATERSON

AGES 10–12

It was up to him [Jess] to pay back to the world in beauty and caring what Leslie had loaned him in vision and strength.

—*Bridge to Terabithia*

Jess Aarons is striving to be the fastest runner in fifth grade at Lark Creek Elementary School. He won the race in fourth grade and became a hero for one day. Jess, an excellent artist, isn't considered a serious athlete; he is just a weird kid who can draw. But, he has not forgotten that sweet taste of winning, and he aims to do it again. Each morning he sprints across the pastures and meadowlands of his family's small farm in rural Virginia, pushing himself harder and harder so that he will be ready on the day of the big race. Then, maybe his father will be proud of him.

The truth is that Jess's father, who works in D.C., has little time to think about his son. He comes home each evening tired from the long commute and expects Jess to have completed all the chores on the farm. Jess's sisters help out around the house, but there are times that Jess feels the burden of being the only son. He craves time to himself, and wishes for a quiet place where he can draw and think. His father disapproves of his art so Jess has no one with whom he can share his drawings except Miss Edmunds, his music teacher. Then, Leslie Burke comes into his life.

Jess meets Leslie for the first time on the day her family moves into the old Perkins place next to his family's farm. There is something different about her, and the kids at school don't take long to notice. The first day of school is the day of the big race, and Leslie shows up to run. No girl has ever raced the boys. "Maybe if he didn't look at her, she would go back to the upper field where she belonged." Does Leslie know that she doesn't belong in the race with the boys? Does she care? Leslie's self-confidence surprises Jess, and the two are in the final race for the championship. "She beat him. She came in first and turned her large shining eyes on a bunch of dumb sweating-mad faces." Jess is humiliated before all the guys at Lark Creek, but he can't help but notice Leslie when she gets off the bus and runs toward the Perkins place. "She ran as though it was her nature. It reminded him of the flight of wild ducks in the autumn. So smooth. The word 'beautiful' came to his mind, but he shook it away and hurried up toward the house."

Jess finally realizes that he will never be the best runner, but something worth more than a championship happens that changes his life. He and Leslie become friends, and the two find a secret hiding place across the creek from their adjoining homes where they create an imaginary kingdom they call Terabithia. "For the first time in his life he got up every morning with something to look forward to. Leslie was more than his friend. She was his other, more exciting self—his way to Terabithia and the worlds beyond." But, Terabithia had to be their secret because if others knew, the magic would be lost forever.

A bit of the magic is lost for Jess when he returns from a museum trip to Washington with Miss Edmunds and finds that Leslie is dead. The rains had caused the creek to swell, and Leslie, in an effort to get to Terabithia, had fallen and hit her head, drowning in the rushing waters. Unable to accept the news of Leslie's death, Jess takes off running. His father, following him in the pickup truck, overtakes Jess and lifts him into his arms, holding him like a baby. At school, Jess is paralyzed with sadness, but Mrs. Myers, his teacher, understands his grief. "He thought about it all day, how before Leslie came, he had been a nothing—a stupid, weird little kid who drew funny pictures and chased around a cow field trying to act big—trying to hide a whole mob of foolish little fears running riot inside his gut."

Jess makes a final trip to Terabithia alone. This time, he makes a wreath of wildflowers and places it on the "carpet of golden needles" in

Leslie's memory. "Father, into Thy hands I commend her spirit." But, there is one more gesture that he must complete. He builds a bridge to Terabithia and carefully leads May Belle, his little sister, across the bridge to the magical kingdom that Leslie helped to create. There, he crowns May Belle Queen of Terabithia. Leslie would be pleased.

Katherine Paterson speaks to her readers because she has a genuine and honest understanding of the realities of life, and she recognizes the importance of fantasy in everyone's world. She tells *Bridge to Terabithia* with compassion, communicating an almost personal relationship with Jess and Leslie. Through the friendship of Jess and Leslie, Katherine Paterson offers vision and beauty to young readers, and promises hope no matter how difficult life may be.

SETTING THE SCENE

Jess Aarons, the main character in *Bridge to Terabithia,* is an artist. He and Leslie, a friend who lives nearby, create an imaginary kingdom. Draw a picture of an imaginary kingdom where you and your best friend may go. What is special about the kingdom that you created?

DISCUSSION

- The emotions of anger, hatred, sadness, love, pride, and jealousy are expressed in the novel. Discuss how Jess deals with each of these emotions.

- What does Leslie mean when she says, "My parents are reassessing their value system"? What are their values? What would Mr. Aarons say his values are?

- How is Jess's relationship with his father different from Leslie's relationship with Bill? Discuss whether Jess is jealous of Leslie's relationship with her father. Why does it bother Jess for Leslie to call her parents by their first names? What does this reveal about her relationship with her parents?

- When Mrs. Myers asks the class to write a composition about their hobby, Jess writes about football even though he hates the game. He knows that if he writes about drawing, everyone will laugh at him. Discuss whether Jess is searching for approval from his classmates, or whether he doesn't know how to deal with disapproval. Why is it sometimes easier to conform? What does Leslie teach Jess about "being himself"?

- Leslie advises Jess about how to handle Janice Avery when she bullies him. "It's the *principle* of the thing, Jess. That's what you've got to understand. You have to stop people like that. Otherwise they turn into tyrants and dictators." Discuss Leslie's advice. Why is Janice Avery such a bully? Leslie and Jess write a note and slip it into Janice Avery's desk. Leslie says, "She deserves everything she gets and then some." Jess doesn't feel exactly the same way toward Janice. Why?

- Jess and Leslie become friends and create the kingdom of Terabithia, but in the beginning, they avoid each other at school. Why do you think they are unwilling to acknowledge their friendship at school?

- Why isn't Jess comfortable having Leslie at his house? Discuss whether he wants to keep their friendship private, or whether his family embarrasses him. What are Mrs. Aarons's feelings about Leslie?

- Jess says that going to Terabithia without Leslie is no good. He needs her "to make the magic." What is magical about Leslie? How does Leslie change Jess?

- Discuss how Jess deals with his grief after Leslie dies. How does Leslie's death change Jess's relationship with his father? How does May Belle recognize Jess's grief?

- The Aarons only go to church on Easter. Leslie's family doesn't go to church at all. Why does Leslie want to go to church with the Aarons? What is the difference between being religious and being spiritual? How is Leslie's family spiritual?

- What is the symbolism in the bridge that Jess builds to cross over to the kingdom of Terabithia?

- *Bridge to Terabithia* has been challenged and removed from the curriculum in schools throughout the United States because of "offensive language," "disrespect of adults," and "an elaborate fantasy world that might lead to confusion." Identify the "offensive language" in the novel. How does this language reflect and identify character? To what are the censors referring when they accuse the book of showing "disrespect of adults"? Why do some adults feel that reading fantasy is unhealthy and confusing? How might fantasy help a person deal with reality in the same way it helps Jess?

ACTIVITIES

- Janice Avery's father beats her. Find out the child abuse laws in your state. In small groups, make a brochure that names and describes the various agencies in your city that help victims of child abuse like Janice Avery. Make the brochures available in the school library.

- Talk about ways to handle bullies. Select a partner and role-play a scene between Jess and Janice Avery. Have Jess deal with Janice in the manner a bully should be handled.

- Terabithia is magical to Leslie and Jess, but Jess doesn't feel that he can draw Terabithia because he can't capture "the poetry of the trees." Leslie assures him, "You will someday." Draw a picture of Terabithia that Jess might draw when he does get "the poetry of the trees."

- Jess has never had to face death until Leslie dies. Sometimes, reading and talking about the grieving process is helpful. Go to the school library and select a novel in which a main character is dealing with the death of a friend or loved one. Write a letter to Jess recommending this novel to him.

- "Jess drew the way some people drink whiskey. The peace would start at the top of his muddled brain and seep down through his tired and tensed-up body." Jess recognizes that art is therapy for him. Research careers in art therapy that Jess might explore. Where might he get training?

- Jess says that he may one day write a letter to Mrs. Myers telling her that Leslie Burke thought she was a good teacher. Why does Jess think this might be important to Mrs. Myers? Write the letter that Jess wants to write.

- Leslie is a good writer and loves language. Locate at least ten poems that Leslie would find especially beautiful. Illustrate each poem, and place them in a booklet for Jess.

- Leslie loves the *Chronicles of Narnia* by C. S. Lewis. She recommends them to Jess. Read these novels, and discuss why they are so important to Leslie. Then, find a passage from one of the books that might be read at Leslie's memorial service.

- Jess expresses himself through art. Draw a series of pictures called "Memories of Leslie" that Jess might send to Mr. and Mrs. Burke.

FICTION CONNECTIONS

Bauer, Marion Dane. *On My Honor.* 1986. 90p. Clarion.

AGES 9–12   Joel must deal with grief and the consequences of disobedience when his best friend drowns in a creek that they had promised never to go near.

Butts, Nancy. *Cheshire Moon.* 1996. 105p. Front Street Press.

AGES 9–12   Miranda is deaf and feels isolated from the normal world. When her best friend dies at sea, she searches for a way to deal with her grief and adjust to the hearing world around her.

Caseley, Judith. *Dorothy's Darkest Days.* 1997. 128p. Greenwillow.

AGES 9–12   Dorothy Kane dislikes Andrea Marino, a classmate who is her partner on a class project. When Andrea is killed in a tragic car accident, Dorothy is overwhelmed with guilt.

Clifford, Eth. *The Remembering Box.* Illustrated by Donna Diamond. 1985. 70p. Houghton Mifflin.

AGES 9–12   Nine-year-old Joshua calls upon his memories of his weekly visits with his grandmother on the Jewish Sabbath to help him accept her death.

Coerr, Eleanor. *Sadako and the Thousand Paper Cranes.* Illustrated by Anne Richardson. 1999. 80p. Puffin.

AGES 9–12   A true story about a young Japanese girl who is hospitalized with leukemia, the "atom bomb disease," and becomes a heroine in Japan when she seeks to verify an old legend that if she folds one thousand paper cranes, the gods will make her healthy.

Conly, Jane Leslie. *What Happened on Planet Kid.* 2000. 216p. Holt.

AGES 9–12   Set in rural Virginia in 1958, two friends, Dawn and Charlotte, create an imaginary world called Planet Kid that is run by girls. When Dawn learns that Charlotte is being abused at home, she must make a decision. Does she tell and risk Charlotte's life? Does she keep the secret and risk her own life?

Couloumbis, Audrey. *Getting Near to Baby.* 1999. 211p. Putnam.

AGES 9–11   Twelve-year-old Willo Jo and her little sister are taken to live with their Aunt Patty when their baby sister dies and their mother lapses into depression. During their stay, they find ways to deal with their grief and get "near to Baby."

Deaver, Julie Reece. *Say Goodnight, Gracie.* 1988. 214p. Harper.

AGES 12–UP   Morgan and Jimmy have been best friends since childhood, and now they share an interest in the arts. When a car accident kills Jimmy, Morgan feels alone and searches for a way to deal with her grief.

Ferris, Jean. *Invincible Summer.* 1994. 176p. Farrar, Straus & Giroux.

AGES 12–UP   Seventeen-year-old Robin is diagnosed with leukemia and meets Rick, a boy who is fighting the same disease. This is a story about love, courage, friendship, and death.

Fletcher, Ralph. *Flying Solo.* 1998. 144p. Clarion.

AGES 9–12   A sixth grade is left to run class themselves when a substitute teacher doesn't show up. By the end of the day, they have managed to deal with their feelings of guilt and sadness about a classmate who died earlier in the year.

Greene, Constance. *Beat the Turtle Drum.* Illustrated by Donna Diamond. 1994 (paperback reprint edition). 128p. Puffin.

AGES 9–12   Thirteen-year-old Katy must deal with the accidental death of her 11-year-old sister.

Hamilton, Virginia. *Cousins.* 1990. 125p. Philomel.

AGES 9–12   Cammy is jealous of her cousin, Patty Ann, and wishes that she would disappear, but when Patty Ann drowns, Cammy's life is filled with the guilt that her wish might have caused Patty Ann's death. An understanding and loving father and grandmother help her in dealing with her grief.

Hurwin, Davida Wills. *A Time for Dancing: A Novel.* 1995. 272p. Little, Brown.

AGES 12–UP   Jules and Sam have been best friends since childhood, share the love of dance, and look forward to attending college together. When Jules discovers that she has cancer, Sam tries to be a good friend, but her fears challenge their friendship, leaving Jules feeling alone.

Katz, Susan. *Snowdrops for Cousin Ruth.* 1998. 128p. Simon & Schuster.

AGES 9–12   When a freak accident takes the life of seven-year-old Johnny, each member of his family grieves in a different way. None of them begins the healing process until elderly Cousin Ruth moves next door and helps them find the way to enjoy life again.

Lowry, Lois. *A Summer to Die.* Illustrated by Jenni Oliver. 1977. 154p. Houghton Mifflin.

AGES 12–UP   Thirteen-year-old Meg has a tough time dealing with her older sister's beauty and popularity, but when Molly becomes seriously ill, Meg's jealousy turns into fear, and the entire family faces the horrible truth that Molly will die.

MacLachlan, Patricia. *Baby.* 1993. 132p. Delacorte.

AGES 9–12   Larkin's family cares for an abandoned baby and, in the process, comes to terms with the earlier death of Larkin's baby brother.

Park, Barbara. *Mick Harte Was Here.* 1995. 89p. Knopf.

AGES 9–12   Thirteen-year-old Phoebe Harte deals with the death of her younger brother by remembering the funny and sometimes annoying things that he used to do.

Smith, Doris Buchanan. *A Taste of Blackberries.* Illustrated by Mike Wimmer. 1992 (reissue). 85p. HarperCollins.

AGES 9–12   Jamie and his best friend are playing in the yard when Jamie is stung by a bee, has an allergic reaction, and dies. Jamie's friend, along with the support of his family and Jamie's family, finds a way to deal with Jamie's death and the thought that he might have saved him.

Warner, Sally. *Sort of Forever.* 1998. 128p. Knopf.

AGES 9–12   Best friends since they were babies, Cady and Nana are looking forward to entering middle school together in the fall, but when Nana is diagnosed with leukemia, Cady demonstrates the true meaning of friendship by sticking by her side until the end.

Whelan, Gloria. *Forgive the River, Forgive the Sky.* 1998. 166p. Wm. B. Eerdmans.

AGES 9–12   When Lily Star's father dies of a heart attack while fishing in the nearby river, Lily blames the river for his death until she meets T.R., a paraplegic former test pilot who blames the sky for his tragic accident. Through each other, they learn to deal with their grief and find a way to go on with their lives.

Yumoto, Kazumi. *The Friends*. Translated by Cathy Hirano. 1996. 170p. Farrar, Straus & Giroux.

AGES 9-12   Three friends become curious about death and spy on an old man whom they think will die soon, but as they watch, they become close to the old man, forming a friendship that changes their lives forever.

I Will Call It Georgie's Blues

Puffin   1983   204 pages

SUZANNE NEWTON

AGES 12–UP

"I hid it from Georgie!" I screamed. "Even though he would have loved it so! I say, I hid it from my brother Georgie, even though he would've loved it so! This is me–Neal Sloan–the real Neal Sloan– and I ain't gonna hide no more!"

–Song sung by Neal Sloan, age 15,
in *I Will Call It Georgie's Blues*

It's tough to keep a secret in a small town where everyone seems to know everything about each other. It's even tougher to keep secrets when your father is a minister and feels that his daily life is under intense scrutiny. But, 15-year-old Neal Sloan manages to keep his secret from his family and the normally observant citizens of Gideon, North Carolina. For two years, he has secretly taken piano lessons and managed to develop his talent for jazz without anyone knowing except his piano teacher, Mrs. Talbot. He knows that his father would never approve of his choice of music for fear that the

Adapted from an article originally published in *Book Links,* March 1998.

congregation of the Gideon Baptist Church would disapprove. Neal, a middle child, prefers to avoid family conflict and, jeopardizing his own identity, dodges his father whenever possible.

Aileen, Neal's older sister, sees things differently. Determined to defy the public image that her father so carefully protects, she hangs out with the town "bum," Pete Cauthlin. At 19 years old, Pete is still trying to finish high school. He is the instigator of almost all fights that erupt on the high school campus, and holds the school suspension record. Though he is forbidden to come near the Sloan home, Aileen claims him as her steady boyfriend and finds ways to be with him. So determined to be a "rebel" herself, Aileen fools around and fails English her senior year in high school. Mr. and Mrs. Sloan are clearly baffled about how to handle their defiant daughter. When her mother confronts her, Aileen quickly replies, "All you care about is that you've got to explain why your bright daughter didn't manage to graduate with others her age. How embarrassing for you!"

Aileen is an embarrassment to her parents, but her problems can be fixed by attending summer school. Seven-year-old Georgie, the youngest Sloan, is in more serious trouble. He is so emotionally disturbed that he loses touch with reality. Neal is the first to notice Georgie's problem. He observes that his little brother is nervous and withdrawn. On several different occasions, Georgie approaches Neal with troubling questions: "Do you think Mom and Dad love me?" "Neal, are you real?" Then, Georgie begins doing strange things. Neal notices that he has a tendency to appear and disappear silently. He goes to a neighborhood grocery store and convinces Mr. Bailey, the owner, to allow him to buy a few canned goods on credit. When Mr. Bailey suggests that Georgie go to his father for money, Georgie tells Mr. Bailey that he can't ask his father because things aren't "good" at home. At this point, rumors begin to spread that Mr. Sloan is emotionally unstable. Determined to get to the bottom of the rumor, Mr. Sloan lashes out at his family.

Neal, who feels protective of his little brother, is at Bailey's store one day and discovers that it was Georgie's conversation with Mr. Bailey that started the rumor about his father. Fearful of what his father might do to Georgie, Neal rushes home to try to explain things. As he enters the front door, Neal realizes that he is too late. His father has made the startling discovery himself, and is bellowing so loudly that Georgie is reduced to silent trembling. In anger, Neal screams that Georgie is sick and "what was making him sick was having to live in the middle of a Great Lie as though nothing was wrong." When Mr. Sloan hears enough, he slaps Neal and instructs him to stay out of the way. Neal scoops Georgie into his arms and removes him from the room. He puts his fragile and silent little brother to bed in the tiny room that he has occupied since his birth. This bedroom, converted from a small storage closet, suddenly symbolizes something to Neal. He realizes that most of Georgie's problem stems from the fact that the Sloan family has "made as little room for Georgie as possible."

Mrs. Sloan is shaken by the entire ordeal. Aware of her husband's position in the community, she has never been willing to make waves, even to protect her children. She has long suspected that Georgie has a problem, and wants to get help. Her fear and concern about her husband's reaction to the issue keep her from approaching him. Instead, she confides in Neal. Though he encourages his mother to discuss the family's problems with his father, Mrs. Sloan remains meek and quiet. Often the pressure of their problems sends her to bed with severe headaches. When Neal finally gets nerve to approach his father, Mr. Sloan responds, "I have responsibilities to an entire congregation. I can't just limit my concerns to the people in my own family."

During this entire time, Mrs. Talbot has served as Neal's friend and confidante. She, who has also lived a life with secrets, encourages Neal to "open up" and talk with his family. She asks him to share his love of music and to stop living a life filled with secrets. Finally, when Georgie disappears and the entire town turns out to look for him, Neal decides that the Sloan family cannot continue hiding. He will insist that they seek help. He vows to himself that if Georgie is found, he will openly and publicly reveal his music by playing a melody that keeps popping into his head—a melody that he calls "Georgie's Blues."

Suzanne Newton's skilled hand weaves a story that reads like the lyrics of a blues song. She never misses a beat, and the rhythm of her writing pulls the reader quickly and gently into the lives of the Sloan family.

SETTING THE SCENE

Discuss the meaning of the phrase "behind closed doors." How does this phrase suggest "secrets"? Talk about the difference between "good secrets" and "bad secrets." Under what condition should someone reveal "bad secrets"?

Play recordings of blues songs. After listening to the lyrics of the songs, discuss why they are called the blues.

DISCUSSION

- What is the irony in the sermon title "Blessed Are the Peacemakers" found on the bulletin board outside the Gideon Baptist Church?

- What does Neal mean when he says to Aileen, "You're cutting off your nose to spite your face"?

- Aileen says, "I want to be a real person, not just somebody's idea of what a preacher's daughter is supposed to be like!" What do you think the people of Gideon expect the Sloan children to be like? Mr. Sloan says that by being a minister, "a person has to give up a great deal!" What do you think he has given up? What has his family given up?

- What is the difference between keeping a secret and "keeping one's business to one's self"? Why does Mrs. Talbot think that it is difficult to keep secrets in Gideon? What is the difference between living a "private life" and being a "fake"?

- Mr. Sloan tells Mr. Mac that Neal will mow the churchyard for free. Neal, on the other hand, decides that he will work only if he is paid. Why is Mr. Sloan's promise to Mr. Mac unfair to Neal?

- Why, do you think, does Mrs. Talbot make Neal go through the motions of asking for piano lessons when she knows how much he wants them? Why, do you think, she agrees to help Neal keep his piano lessons a secret?

- Discuss why Mrs. Talbot waits so long before telling Neal about her husband.

- Neal sits outside Mrs. Talbot's door while she gives a piano lesson to a young student: "It seemed to me that bad playing would be more bearable than going home to face another kind of music." To what other kind of music is Neal referring?

- What is Neal's perception of his mother? Compare and contrast Mrs. Sloan with Mrs. Talbot. Why is Neal more comfortable at Mrs. Talbot's house?

- Neal feels humiliated when his father makes him stop outside the church and shake hands with him. Find other scenes in the book in which Neal feels humiliated.

- Describe Neal's relationship with Georgie. At what point does Neal realize that Georgie has serious emotional problems? What physical evidence is there that Georgie is a disturbed child? What is the first clue that there is little room in the Sloan family for Georgie? What does Neal mean when he says that Georgie is the "everlasting scape-goat" of the Sloan family?

- Mrs. Talbot says to Neal, "Our friendship keeps you from trying to be friends with your own folks." Do you think that most teenagers really want to be friends with their parents? How important is it for young people to have an adult friend?

- Neal says that in his family "every subject leads to tears and shouting, or else silence, which is worse." Why is talking over problems better than remaining silent?

- Though there is no current recorded challenge to *I Will Call It Georgie's Blues*, some parents have objected to the language that Neal uses and to the way the minister's family is presented. What is Neal trying to accomplish when he uses profanity in the novel? How is his use of profane language a good way to get his mother's attention? Discuss the reasons why someone might object to the way the Sloan family is presented. Why should we assume that a minister's family is immune from problems? How can we ever really know what goes on "behind closed doors" in someone's family? How does the ending of the novel reveal that there is hope for the Sloan family?

ACTIVITIES

- Write a note that Georgie might have left his family on the day he disappeared.

- Write a journal entry that Aileen might have written on the day her parents discovered that she wasn't going to graduate from high school.

- Music can express a person's deepest emotions. Neal is writing a jazz piece that he calls "Georgie's Blues." Select a character from the book and write the lyrics for a blues song about that character.

- Draw a caricature of a famous jazz musician. Mount the drawing on black construction paper and attach a photocopied picture of the musician. Share your drawing with the class and briefly tell the person's contribution to the world of jazz. If possible, share a recording of the person's music.

- Conduct a taped interview with a minister's kid, a teacher's kid, or a public official's kid. Ask them to describe the advantages and disadvantages of being a child of a parent involved in public service. Do their parents have special expectations of them? Do their peers treat them differently? What advice would they give others in their situation?

- Masks are worn either to hide or to reveal something about a person. Using papier-mâché, make an appropriate mask for one of the characters in the novel.

- Research places in your city or community that might provide help for emotionally disturbed children and their families. Make a brochure briefly describing the agencies and the services they offer. Include addresses and telephone numbers. Share the brochure with the class and tell which agency you would recommend to the Sloan family.

- At the end of the novel, Neal reveals his piano-playing talent. Design a program for his first piano recital. Include an acknowledgment to Mrs. Talbot.

- Read *The Language of Goldfish* by Zibby O'Neal (Puffin, 1990). Compare Carrie's love of art and the help she receives from her art teacher with Neal's love of music and the help he receives from Mrs. Talbot. Stage a scene in which Carrie and Neal meet. What kinds of things might they discuss?

FICTION CONNECTIONS

Angell, Judie. *The Buffalo Nickel Blues Band.* 1982. 183p. Bradbury, o.p.

AGES 9–12   Eddie Levy and his friends form a jazz band and, with the help of his mother, find an audience.

Bontemps, Arna. *Lonesome Boy.* 1955. 28p. Houghton Mifflin, o.p.

AGES 8–11   Bubber carries his trumpet everywhere and dreams of becoming as great a jazz player as his idol, Louis Armstrong.

Collier, James Lincoln. *The Jazz Kid.* 1994. 216p. Holt.

AGES 10–12   Twelve-year-old Paulie Horvath isn't a good student like his brother, but he is addicted to jazz, which he hears from the basement of a speakeasy in his Chicago neighborhood. His growing desire to play like King Oliver and Louis Armstrong brings disapproval from his family and causes him to face some difficult decisions regarding his future.

Curtis, Christopher Paul. *Bud, Not Buddy.* 1999. 245p. Delacorte.

AGES 10–14   Growing up in 1936 in Flint, Michigan, Bud, an orphan, sets out in search of his father. His father's identity was a well-kept secret by his mother, but Bud uses clues from some old band flyers to lead him in the direction of the truth.

Marino, Jan. *The Day That Elvis Came to Town.* 1991. 204p. Little, Brown.

AGES 12–UP   In this novel set in the South in the early sixties, Mercedes Washington, a glamorous jazz singer, takes a room in a boarding house, where she promises young Wanda a chance to meet Elvis Presley. While Wanda faces much disappointment, Mercedes does help her come face-to-face with hidden truths about herself and her family.

Matthews, Kezi. *Joh Riley's Daughter.* 2000. 122p. Front Street.

AGES 10–UP   Thirteen-year-old Memphis is still waiting for her father who left her at her grandmother's house in South Carolina sometime back, and she is dealing with the knowledge that she may have been the person to cause her retarded Aunt Clover to walk away from home. During this troubling time, Memphis finds solace in playing her guitar.

Paterson, Katherine. *Flip-Flop Girl.* 1994. 120p. Lodestar/Dutton.

AGES 9–12   Nine-year-old Vinnie and her five-year-old brother, Mason, move with their mom to Virginia to live with their grandma after their dad is killed. Mason hasn't talked since his father died, but the family can hardly believe that the help they need comes from Lupe, the flip-flop girl.

Quattlebaum, Mary. *Jazz, Pizzazz and the Silver Threads.* Illustrated by Robin Oz. 1996. 112p. Delacorte.

AGES 9–12   A humorous story about 9-year-old Calvin Hastings and a host of other characters who use their love of jazz, and a hamster named Pizzazz that does magic tricks, to enter the world of showbiz.

NONFICTION CONNECTIONS

Awmiller, Craig. *This House on Fire: The Story of the Blues.* 1995. 160p. Watts.

AGES 10–UP   This volume in the African-American Experience series presents an overview of the blues as a musical genre that has grown out of the rich musical heritage of African Americans. It includes biographical sketches of famous blues musicians and discusses how their music has influenced other forms of contemporary music.

Carlin, Richard. *Jazz*. 1991. 142p. Facts on File.

AGES 12–UP   This entry in the World of Music series discusses the history of jazz from its rich beginnings, revealing its musical elements and the people who made it a legitimate musical form.

Collier, James Lincoln. *Jazz: An American Saga*. 1997. 104p. Holt.

AGES 10–UP   Through this history of jazz, readers learn about the beginnings of the jazz movement and meet the musicians who introduced jazz to the American public

David, Ron. *Jazz for Beginners*. 1995. 156p. Documentary Beginners Comic Books.

AGES 10–UP   David includes biographies of the greatest jazz musicians and traces the development of jazz from the early part of the twentieth century to today's bebop, Dixieland, and jazz-rock.

Feather, Leonard. *From Satchmo to Miles*. 1972. 258p. Da Capo.

AGES 12–UP   Twelve well-known jazz artists are featured as the musicians responsible for the development of jazz in the twentieth century.

Gottlieb, William P. *The Golden Age of Jazz*. 1995. 162p. Pomegranate Art Books.

AGES 12–UP   More than 200 photographs document the "Golden Age of Jazz," the 1930s through the 1940s, revealing the people and places that were a major part of this particular jazz era.

Gourse, Leslie. *Swingers and Crooners: The Art of Jazz Singing*. 1997. 144p. Watts.

AGES 12–UP   The rich history of jazz singing, which came of age in the early twentieth century with such greats as Louis Armstrong, Bessie Smith, and Ma Rainey, is traced to the work songs of slaves and the gospels and spirituals of African American churches. Also discussed in this volume from the Art of Jazz series are the popularity of contemporary experimental jazz and the importance of this musical genre among today's music lovers.

Haskins, James. *Black Music in America: A History through Its People.* 1987. 224p. HarperCollins/Crowell

AGES 12–UP   Haskins discusses the many musical forms enjoyed and created by African Americans, including jazz and the blues.

Hughes, Langston. *The Dream Keeper and Other Poems.* Illustrated by Helen Sewell. 1986. 80p. Knopf, o.p.

AGES 12–UP   This collection of 59 poems is divided into five sections and includes lyrical poems and blues songs, many that reflect the African American experience.

Hughes, Langston. *The First Book of Jazz.* Illustrated by Cliff Roberts. Music selected by David Martin. 1995. 73p. Ecco Press.

AGES 10–UP   A well-known African American writer tells the history of jazz and how this style of music contributed to his work as a poet.

Mjorgenstern, Dan. *Jazz People.* 1993. 300p. Da Capo.

AGES 12–UP   Originally published by Abrams in 1976, this history of jazz presents "the giants of jazz" and discusses the long climb they faced before their music was accepted as an art form.

Monceaux, Morgan. *Jazz; My Music, My People.* 1994. 64p. Knopf.

AGES 10–UP   Monceaux traces the development of jazz music, the early years, the swing years, bebop, and modern jazz, through brief vignettes of black jazz musicians.

Oliver, Paul. *The Story of the Blues.* 1969. 176p. Chilton, o.p.

AGES 12–UP   More than 500 photographs and drawings and blues lyrics are used to present this history of the blues.

Seymour, Gene. *Jazz: The Great American Art.* 1995. 160p. Watts.

AGES 12–UP   Seymour traces the growth of jazz from its beginnings as slave songs to its more contemporary versions in the form of the blues, ragtime, and swing.

Shadwick, Keith. *The Illustrated Story of Jazz.* 1991. 181p. Book Sales.

AGES 12–UP   Shadwick traces the history of jazz from past to present and discusses the personalities that have been credited with making this type of music an American phenomenon.

Terkel, Studs. *Giants of Jazz*. 1975. 210p. HarperCollins/Crowell.

AGES 12–UP   The development of jazz as a musical form that "belongs to everybody" is traced through the life stories of 13 of the greatest jazz artists.

Vigna, Giuseppe. *Jazz and Its History*. Illustrated by Studio Boni-Pieri-Critone. 1999. 64p. Barrons.

AGES 9–12   Performers like Louis Armstrong, Duke Ellington, Miles Davis, Thelonius Monk, and numerous other jazz musicians are featured in this book that discusses jazz as one of America's greatest forms of music.

Williams, Richard. *Jazz: A Photographic Documentary*. 1994. 144p. Random, o.p.

AGES 12–UP   Black-and-white photographs document the jazz greats on and offstage, revealing the passion and creativity that they have given to their music.

STRATEGY 10

The Giver

Houghton Mifflin   1993   180 pages

LOIS LOWRY

AGES 10–UP

I'm grateful to you, Jonas, because without you I would never have figured out a way to bring about the change. But your role now is to escape. And my role is to stay.

—*The Giver*

In this 1994 Newbery Medal winner, Lois Lowry presents a thought-provoking look at a future society through one of its youngest members, 12-year-old Jonas. The well-crafted narrative begins with Jonas's "apprehension" over the upcoming Ceremony of Twelves in which he will receive his Assignment, or occupation, from the esteemed Committee of Elders: "It was almost December, and Jonas was beginning to be frightened."

Despite his concerns, Jonas's orderly and predictable life seems pleasant enough, one might even say appealing. He has patient and understanding parents, an engaging younger sister, and close friends. The minor conflicts

---

This strategy is adapted from an article by Julie Corsaro in *Book Links,* May 1994.

in his life are quickly resolved through the daily sharing of feelings at dinnertime and the telling of dreams in the morning. The pain that accompanies his childhood bumps and scrapes is quickly alleviated with readily available medication. While there are many rules and punishments governing Jonas's life, these seem rather benign. For instance, the punishment for bragging and rudeness (considered one of the worst offenses) is "gentle chastisement."

When Jonas is selected to be the next Receiver of Memory, however, the problems hinted at in the shadows of his efficient, antiseptic world come out. Under the guidance of his teacher—the former Receiver of Memory and the new Giver—Jonas is initially offered memories of pleasant things, such as snow, sunshine, and color, that existed before his community turned to Sameness. As a result, he begins to question his community's lack of freedom: "If everything's the same, then there aren't any choices! I want to wake up in the morning and decide things!" Jonas's teacher also gives him the startling and disturbing images of war, starvation, poverty, and cruelty, which also existed before his community eliminated difference. When Jonas asks, "Why can't everyone have the memories? I think it would seem a little easier if the memories were shared," The Giver tells him, "That's the real reason The Receiver is so vital to them, and so honored. They selected me—and you—to lift that burden from themselves."

After The Giver shares his favorite memory, an extended family's warm and joyful Christmas celebration, Jonas questions the composition of his own family, a nonbiological "unit" that has been carefully planned and regulated by the community. Jonas comes to the realization that depth of human feelings and emotions is impossible without the existence of memories and traditions, inner turmoil, and outer struggle. This concept is vividly reinforced when he asks his parents if they love him, and, chuckling, his mother responds, "You used a very generalized word, so meaningless that it's become obsolete."

Although Jonas initially feels helpless to change life in the community, he seriously reconsiders after The Giver tells him what happened 10 years earlier when a Receiver-in-Training was "released" and her memories went out into the community, creating chaos. After watching a videotape the following day showing his father's "release" of a baby twin, Jonas is horrified to learn that this commonly used term is actually a euphemism for planned killing. More determined than ever, he and The Giver come up with a courageous plan: they will spend the next two weeks preparing for Jonas to run away, thus forcing the community to bear the memories he will leave behind.

However, when Jonas returns home later that evening, he learns that Gabriel, the "newchild" his family has spent the year caring for, will be released the following morning. Before daybreak, Jonas and Gabriel escape, embarking on a dangerous journey to Elsewhere, the unknown world outside the community. Their ultimate fate is uncertain.

ON UTOPIAS AND DYSTOPIAS

The setting of *The Giver* is a dystopia, literally meaning "bad place." In order to gain some understanding of this genre, one needs to be familiar with its optimistic rival, the utopia ("no place"). While the utopian narrative in the West can be traced back to Plato's *Republic*, the term *utopia* itself derives from Sir Thomas More's famous work of 1516, *Utopia*, in which he attacked the social, cultural, and political evils of his day and then described an ideal island community, which he named Utopia. From Francis Bacon's *The New Atlantis* (1627), the genre tended to contrast a perfect future state with a less-desirable present one. The nineteenth-century speculative works of H. G. Wells figure prominently in the twentieth-century response to the utopia and the rise of its literary inversion, the dystopia. While Wells advocated a visionary paradise based on technological achievements (remember that climate control and genetic engineering have significance in *The Giver*), such writers as Aldous Huxley (*Brave New World*, 1934) and George Orwell (*1984*, 1949) responded to the potential threat of uncontrolled advances in science and technology and the political reality of totalitarian regimes.

According to Robert S. Baker in *Brave New World: History, Science and Dystopia* (Twayne, 1990), utopian and dystopian narratives are structured around a series of polarities that inform each genre. Rationality and logic, controlled nature, science, community, self-renunciation and service, limited or no sexuality, superior communication, and social harmony: these are the principal conventions of the utopian genre. In contrast, feeling, emotion, and instinct; primitive nature; religion; the individual; self-assertion; sensual pleasure; debased language; and social conflict are extolled as virtues in the dystopian genre. Advanced students will want to research and then discuss how *The Giver* fits in among these principal themes.

SETTING THE SCENE

Before reading *The Giver*, ask students to write a utopian narrative or invent a utopia and describe it in writing. When they have finished the book, and keeping in mind the quote "We gained control of many things, but we had to let go of others," have them change their utopia into a dystopia.

DISCUSSION

- "It was one of the rituals, the evening telling of feelings." What are the other rituals or rules that Jonas must follow before the Ceremony of Twelves? How do these compare with the rules you are expected to follow at home, school, church, or temple?

- During the Ceremony of Twelves, Jonas's friends Fiona and Asher are given their Life Assignments. If you attended a similar ceremony today, what assignment, or job, do you think you would receive from your elders? Why? Would you choose the same job for yourself?

- Describe Jonas's relationship with his family and friends. How does his "selection" change that? What would you think of Asher and Fiona if they were your friends?

- The Giver's favorite memory is of "families, and holidays, and happiness." If you could give Jonas your favorite memory, what would it be? How is yours similar to or different from The Giver's?

- Jonas lives in a community that has turned to Sameness. Are there times in your life when you choose sameness or conformity? What are they? When do you act independently?

- When Jonas asks, "What if we could hold up things that were bright red or bright yellow, and [Gabriel] could choose?" The Giver responds, "He might make wrong choices." What are the advantages and disadvantages of having choices? Have you ever made a wrong one? Have you ever regretted having to choose?

- When The Giver shows Jonas the videotape of his father's release of the baby twin, is he trying to be honest and open, or is he hoping Jonas will leave the community, thus releasing his memories?

ACTIVITIES

- Read the biblical story of the archangel Gabriel in the New Testament. What is significant about the name of the condemned baby in *The Giver?*

- Read Aylette Jenness's *Families: A Celebration of Diversity, Commitment and Love* (Houghton, 1990). How do the contemporary families profiled in this book compare with your own family? With Jonas's family?

- Interview your grandparents or other senior citizens about their favorite family traditions and memories. How are these similar to or different from your own?

- Select a Committee of Elders from among your classmates. Have them choose "Assignments" for the rest of the class and impose rules related to Sameness to be followed for one day. On the next, discuss what you and your classmates thought and felt about the assignments and rules.

- Population is controlled in Jonas's society through family planning (one boy and one girl per household) and the euphemistic "release" of the old, difficult babies, twins, and individuals who break the rules. Using current periodicals and books (titles in the Opposing Viewpoints series [Greenhaven] will be particularly useful for this assignment), research current means of controlling the number of people living on our planet. Then, dividing into pro and con teams, debate such related issues as euthanasia, genetic engineering, and state-enforced birth control.

- Jonas never wrote a letter to his family and friends before he ran away. Write a letter that Jonas might have written trying to explain why he left the community.

- Discuss the dust jacket. Design a cover showing either your favorite scene or an image that you think suggests the novel's theme or philosophy.

FICTION CONNECTIONS

Bomans, Godfried. *Eric in the Land of the Insects.* Translated from the Dutch by Regina Louise Kornblith. Illustrated by Mark Richardson. 1994. 196p. Houghton Mifflin.

AGES 10–UP   When he jumps into a landscape painting bustling with insects, Eric is surprised to meet animals concerned with such "human" issues as money, religion, and morality.

Bunyan, John. *Pilgrim's Progress*. Retold by James Reeves. Illustrated by Joanna Troughton. 1987. 160p. Peter Bedrick.

AGES 12–UP An accessible update of the seventeenth-century allegory about the Pilgrim's heroic journey from the City of Destruction to the Celestial City.

Burleigh, Robert. *A Man Named Thoreau*. Illustrated by Lloyd Bloom. 1985. 48p. Atheneum.

AGES 10–12 By skillfully interweaving quotes from Walden with biographical information, Burleigh creates a vivid picture of the philosopher who celebrated individualism and harmony between humans and nature.

Christopher, John. *The White Mountains*. 1967. 192p. Macmillan.

AGES 12–UP Before they turn 14 and are "capped" by despotic machine creatures called Tripods, Will and his friends undertake a daring escape to a free colony in the White Mountains.

George, Jean Craighead. *My Side of the Mountain*. 1988. 176p. Dutton.

AGES 9–12 Sam, 14, runs away from New York City and spends a year living alone in a mountain wilderness.

Lisle, Janet Taylor. *Forest*. 1993. 160p. Orchard/Richard Jackson.

AGES 10–UP After a 12-year-old girl innocently spends a night in the giant oaks of the Upper Forest, the mink-tail squirrels are certain that an attack by humans is under way.

Lowry, Lois. *Gathering Blue*. 2000. 215p. Houghton Mifflin.

AGES 10–UP Kira, lame since birth, is considered flawed by the community, but her life is saved when the Council of Guardians appoints her to restore the robe worn at the annual Ruin Song Gathering.

Nelson, O. T. *The Girl Who Owned a City*. 1995. 200p. Runestone Press.

AGES 10–UP A deadly plague hits the city and kills everyone over the age of 12, leaving the city to be run by the children. Ten-year-old Lisa emerges as the leader, but the task is almost too much for her.

O'Brien, Robert C. *Z for Zachariah*. 1975. 156p. Atheneum.

AGES 10–UP Teenage Ann is frightened when she discovers that John—the other survivor of a nuclear war—killed his previous companion.

Pullman, Philip. *The Amber Spyglass.* 2000 544p. Knopf.

AGES 12–UP   Lyra and Will continue to travel through the mysterious otherworld where they rendezvous with wheeled creatures with the power to see Dust; but, the most haunting discovery is the power of Dr. Malone's amber spyglass, and the names of who will live and who will die. (Book 3 of His Dark Materials trilogy)

Pullman, Philip. *The Golden Compass.* 1996. 399p. Knopf.

AGES 12–UP   Lyra witnesses an assassination attempt against her uncle and is pulled into a frightening adventure that takes her to the cold, far North where she encounters Gobblers and stolen children, witch clans, and armored bears. (Book 1 of His Dark Materials trilogy)

Pullman, Philip. *The Subtle Knife.* 1997. 326p. Knopf.

AGES 12–UP   Lyra meets Will Parry, a fugitive boy from a third universe, and together they travel to Cittagazze, a haunted otherworld where they uncover a secret and come face-to-face with their own destiny. (Book 2 of His Dark Materials trilogy)

Silverberg, Robert. *Letters from Atlantis.* 1990. 144p. Atheneum.

AGES 12–UP   When a twenty-first-century time traveler enters the consciousness of a prince of Atlantis, he wonders how such a glittering civilization can exist alongside the barbarism of Stone Age Europe.

STRATEGY 11

Julie of the Wolves

HarperCollins   1972   170 pages

JEAN CRAIGHEAD GEORGE

AGES 10-14

She [Julie] stepped forward on the vast stage at the top of the world and bowed to her immense audience.

—Julie of the Wolves

The Eskimo culture is rich with tradition and superstition. These Arctic people are naturalists and conservationists. Many of them live by the values and ways of their ancestors, and practice some of the traditional customs. Some of them have adopted more American ways. Jean Craighead George writes about this conflict of culture in *Julie of the Wolves*. This highly acclaimed novel was the winner of the 1973 Newbery Medal and is considered a modern children's classic.

Left by Kapugen, her widowed father, when she was very young, Miyax, whose American name is Julie, lives with her Aunt Martha until she turns 13, when she is expected to marry Daniel, the son of Naka, an Eskimo who practices "old-time" traditions. It is June when Miyax gets the word from the head of Indian Affairs in Mekoryuk that she is to go to Daniel. "You are now thirteen . . . and I have in my files an agreement for this arrangement signed by Kapugen and Naka." When Aunt Martha explains to Miyax that she can refuse the arrangement, Miyax replies, "The old ways are best." She takes leave of her beloved Aunt Martha and boards a plane to fly to Barrow, Alaska, where she will meet Daniel for the first time. There are fleeting moments in flight when Miyax has misgivings about her future, but she is committed to keeping her father's arrangement. Then, she sees Daniel. "She knew from his grin and dull eyes that something was wrong with him." Nusan, Daniel's mother, sees Miyax's disappointment, and says, "Daniel has a few problems. . . . But he's a very good boy, and he's a good worker. He cleans the animal cages at the research lab. He will be like a brother to you."

Miyax doesn't mind the idea of a brother, but to her surprise there is a wedding planned for the next day. Unhappy and confused, she desperately wants a letter from her pen pal in San Francisco and dreams of becoming "Julie" and adopting an American way of life. How can she be a wife to this dull boy who mumbles to himself and tinkers with his radio? Pearl Norton, a married girl Miyax's age, assures her, "All you have to do is leave the house or run away and everything's forgotten. Most of these arrangements are for convenience." But, Miyax's situation gets worse when Daniel comes home in a rage because the guys are laughing at him. "Ha, ha. Dumb Daniel. He's got a wife and he can't mate her. Ha." In an unsuccessful attempt to "mate" Miyax, Daniel leaves in anger, vowing, "Tomorrow, tomorrow I can, I can, can, can, ha ha." This unpleasant encounter with Daniel finally gives Miyax the courage to escape "her Eskimo culture" and begin the search for a new life.

In her journey to find a home, Miyax becomes lost on the Alaskan tundra and discovers that the only way she can survive is to become friends with a pack of Arctic wolves. She remembers that Kapugen had said that wolves are "brotherly" if you learn their language. Her intelligence and her genuine love for the wolves gains her acceptance among the wolf pack, and eventually leads Miyax to rethink her Eskimo heritage and her place in the old culture.

Finally, Miyax comes upon a hunter and his wife who lead her to Kangik, where she finds Kapugen and his gussak (Eskimo for "Caucasian") wife. Their home is filled with modern conveniences like electric lamps, a radio-phonograph, an electric stove, a coffeepot, and china dishes. But, the most troubling discovery is Kapugen's new way of hunting. "I now own an airplane, Miyax. It's the only way to hunt today. The seals are scarce, and whales are almost gone; but sportsmen can still hunt from the plane." Is this the same man who practiced the "old ways" and arranged for her to marry Daniel? Troubled by Kapugen's new life, Miyax firmly states that "she is Eskimo, and as an Eskimo she must live." But, when circumstances cause her to realize that "the hour of the wolf and the Eskimo is over," Miyax makes a decision to become Julie and return to a life with Kapugen.

In 1994, Jean Craighead George published *Julie*, the sequel to *Julie of the Wolves*, and in 1997, the twenty-fifth anniversary of *Julie of the Wolves*, George gave young readers the gift of a third book, *Julie's Wolf Pack*.

In *Julie*, Miyax has survived the tundra with the help of her wolves, and now she must find a way to help them survive. Kapugen has given up many of the Eskimo traditions, and as head of the village's corporation, Kapugen pledges to kill the wolves if they threaten the musk oxen, the livelihood of the community. Determined to convince her father that the wolves must be saved, Julie sets out on a mission that not only saves the wolves but changes her life as well.

Julie's Wolf Pack returns readers to the tundra, where the story continues—told from the wolves' point of view. The lives of the wolves are once again threatened. This time, Julie's beloved wolves face disease and famine. Kapu, the young, inexperienced leader of the pack, must find a way to protect the wolves while defending his leadership position from rival wolves that are waiting to ambush him and take over the pack. The survival of Julie's wolves depends upon Kapu's strength and his ability to maintain his leadership post and unite his pack.

Julie of the Wolves is a unique coming-of-age story that raises important questions about belonging and self-identity. Though the culture may be foreign to many young readers, they will leave the novel with an understanding that the process of growing and changing transcends all cultures.

SETTING THE SCENE

Various cultures and religions have formal coming-of-age ceremonies when a girl and a boy reach a certain age. At one time, in the Eskimo culture, a girl was expected to marry at the age of 13. Have students find out how other cultures celebrate coming-of-age. Discuss these rituals and ceremonies in class.

DISCUSSION

- *Julie of the Wolves* is divided into three parts: Part 1, Amaroq, the wolf; Part 2, Miyax, the girl; and Part 3, Kapugen, the hunter. Discuss the significance of each part to the overall conflict of the book.

- Miyax's English name is Julie. She didn't mind when the children from Mekoryuk called her Julie. She didn't even mind when her mother called her by her English name. Why does she mind when her father, Kapugen, calls her Julie?

- "Miyax knew when to stop dreaming and be practical." What are Miyax's dreams? At what times must she be practical?

- How does Miyax know that she can learn to communicate with the wolves? How does she teach the wolf language? What makes her choose the black wolf to communicate with first? Why does she think he possesses "wisdom"?

- Miyax says that Amaroq is "clearly the wealthy wolf." How does she define *wealthy*? How does she know that Amaroq is the leader of the wolf pack? Find evidence that he is indeed wealthy by Miyax's definition.

- What does Miyax mean when she says that Jello's actions are "the manner of the lone wolf"?

- What does Julie mean when she says, "Daylight is spelled A-M-Y"?

- "Miyax had felt the bleakness of being left behind once before." Relate the times that Miyax feels "left behind." How does her choice in the end make her feel "left behind" once again?

- What does Miyax mean when she says, "My own Amaroq lives. I must go to him!"?

- "[Kapugen] had been dead to her for so long that she was almost frightened by the knowledge that he lived. Yet she loved each cold chill that told her it was true." Why do you think Miyax is frightened when she learns that her father is still alive? How does she still need him? At the end of the novel, "Julie pointed her boots toward Kapugen." How does this decision help to resolve her conflict?

- Why does Julie say, "The hour of the wolf and the Eskimo is over"?

- In the Eskimo c   e, as in many other cultures, turning 13 means marriage. What does turning 13 mean in our society? What responsibilities do you gain upon turning 13? How can family structure affect the age at which one receives and accepts responsibility?

- *Julie of the Wolves* has been challenged in many schools because of the "attempted rape scene." Discuss why Daniel's attempt to "mate" Julie might be considered violent in the eyes of some readers. Talk about whether Daniel means to be rough with Julie. Discuss how the scene might have been different had Daniel been of normal intelligence. How does this scene ultimately change Julie's life?

ACTIVITIES

- Jean Craighead George uses similes to create certain images (for example, "the puppies' playground was speckled with bones like tombstones in a graveyard"). Find other examples of similes in the book.

- Write a letter that Julie might have written to her pen pal, Amy, about her life with the wolves.

- "The old Eskimo customs are not so foolish—they have purpose." Make a list of all the Eskimo customs that Miyax practices. Then, draw a mural reflecting these customs.

- Kapugen arranges Miyax's marriage to Daniel. Research marriage customs of other cultures that you have studied. Share the information that you find with your class. Discuss how these customs differ from the marriage customs of our society.

- "The fur captured her warm breath, held it against her face, and she became her own radiant stove." Use books in the library or search the Internet to find out the proper way to dress in an Arctic climate. Write and illustrate a short brochure for tourists on the proper way to dress when traveling to Alaska.

- On January 24, "the Eskimos lifted their arms and turned their palms to the source of all life." What is the significance of this date? Find other important events that the Eskimos celebrate. Using a sheet of poster board, create a picture of one special event. On the back, write a paragraph explaining the significance of the special day and the way it is celebrated.

- Fairy tales and folktales often portray wolves as bad. Write Julie's story as a folktale, portraying the wolf as a "hero" rather than a "villain."

- "The fur of the fox changes each season to match the color of the land." Go to the library and research other animals that change with the season. Write a short paper entitled "Nature's Way of Protecting Animals."

- "Birds and animals all had languages and if you listened and watched them you could learn about their enemies, where their food lay and when big storms were coming." Select one animal mentioned in the book and research the communication skills of this animal. Write an article entitled "Talking with the Animals" for a science magazine.

- Miyax tries to guess the date by watching the dipping sun. Find out how travelers can tell the date by the sun. Draw a diagram showing the position of the sun the second week in August. Share your information and diagram with the class.

- "The guidepost of her ancestors, the North Star, would soon be visible and would point her way when the birds had all gone south." Find out how Native Americans used the North Star and other heavenly bodies to guide them. Draw a celestial map labeling the North Star and other significant constellations.

- Many string games that children enjoy today originated with the Inuit Eskimos. Using Camilla Gryski's *Cat's Cradle, Owl's Eyes* (Morrow, 1984), learn a string game unique to the Inuit culture and demonstrate it to the class. Share the superstitions that the Inuit had about the game.

- Miyax would often make up rhymes about the tundra and sing them to familiar tunes. "She sang about the wolves, her house, and the little feather flower on her table." Select a familiar tune and write lyrics that Miyax might have sung. Share the song with the class.

FICTION CONNECTIONS

Craig, Ruth. *Malu's Wolf.* 1995. 192p. Orchard.

AGES 9–12   Malu, a young Cro-Magnon girl, raises a young wolf pup when the mother is killed, and tension builds when Gunto, a young hunter, provokes the wolf. When the wolf bites him, Gunto demands that it be killed.

Easley, Maryann. *I Am the Ice Worm.* 1996. 128p. Boyds Mills Press.

AGES 9–12   Fourteen-year-old Allison is en route to visit her mother in Alaska when her plane crashes. Rescued by a hunter, Allison lives and travels with Inupiat Alaskans and quickly learns the value of their culture.

George, Jean Craighead. *Arctic Son.* Illustrated by Wendell Minor. 1997. 32p. Hyperion.

AGES 8–10   The people of a small Inupiat Eskimo village near the Arctic Ocean welcome Luke, a white boy, into their culture by granting him the Eskimo name Kupaaq.

George, Jean Craighead. *Water Sky*. 1987. 212p. HarperCollins.

AGES 10–UP   Lincoln Noah Stonewright leaves the comforts of his Massachusetts home to spend a few months at a whaling camp in Barrow, Alaska, where he begins exploring his own Eskimo heritage.

Hall, Elizabeth. *Child of the Wolves*. 1996. 160p. Houghton Mifflin.

AGES 10–UP   A Siberian husky puppy escapes a kennel and is alone in the Alaskan wilderness until Snowdrift, a great white wolf, invites him into the pack.

Heinz, Brian J. *Kayuktuk: An Arctic Quest*. Illustrated by Jon Van Zyle. 1996. 40p. Chronicle.

AGES 8–UP   Aknik, an Inupiat Eskimo, is forbidden to hunt the bowhead whale with the men of the village because he fails to bring back meat from his snares.

Houston, James. *Drifting Snow: An Arctic Search*. 1992. 160p. Macmillan/Margaret K. McElderry.

AGES 12–UP   Separated from her Inuit family when she was a small child, Elizabeth returns as an adolescent to search for her family and to reclaim her heritage.

Houston, James. *The Falcon Bow: An Arctic Legend*. 1986. 96p. Macmillan/Margaret K. McElderry.

AGES 12–UP   Kungo and his sister bring about peace and understanding between the Inuit and the inland Indians when both societies are struggling for food.

Houston, James. *Ice Swords: An Undersea Adventure*. 1985. 149p. Atheneum.

AGES 12–UP   Matthew, a white boy, and his Inuit friend, Kayak, spend the summer working with an American scientist at an Arctic research station. Suspense and danger unite the two cultures. Also, note Houston's *Frozen Fire* and *Black Diamonds* (both Atheneum).

Hoyt-Goldsmith, Diane. *Arctic Hunter*. Illustrated by Lawrence Migdale. 1992. 30p. Holiday House.

AGES 8–UP   Reggie, a 10-year-old Inupiat Eskimo, describes the camp in Alaska where his family spends each summer hunting and fishing for foods that will last them through the winter months.

Luenn, Nancy. *Arctic Unicorn*. 1986. 168p. Atheneum.

AGES 12–UP   Kala, a 13-year-old girl who resists the special powers that make her a shaman, must choose between the old ways and the new for the sake of her people.

Meyer, Carolyn. *In a Different Light: Growing Up in a Yup'ik Eskimo Village in Alaska*. Photographs by John McDonald. 1996. 181p. Simon & Schuster.

AGES 11–14   The fictionalized Eskimo village of Chaputnguak, Alaska, is the setting for this story about how changes caused by technology are replacing the old skills of the Yupik people.

Newth, Mette. *The Abduction*. 1989. 256p. Farrar, Straus & Giroux.

AGES 12–UP   Near Greenland, Osuqo, an Inuit Eskimo, is traveling with her people to their summer home when she and Poq, the boy she is to marry, are abducted. The young Inuit couple is taken to Norway where they are thrown into a filthy dungeon and put on display as freaks.

O'Dell, Scott. *Black Star, Bright Dawn*. 1988. 134p. Houghton Mifflin.

AGES 12–UP   When her father is injured, Bright Dawn, an Inuit girl, faces the challenge of the Iditarod dog sled race alone.

Patent, Dorothy Hinshaw. *Return of the Wolf*. 1995. 67p. Clarion.

AGES 9–12   Hunting is difficult for Sedra, a lone wolf, until she meets Jasper, another loner. The two become mates and begin to form a pack.

Vanasse, Deb. *A Distant Enemy*. 1997. 192p. Lodestar.

AGES 11–14   Fourteen-year-old Joseph, a Yupik Eskimo, is angry because white intruders are threatening his people's ways in the remote southwestern Alaska town where he lives.

NONFICTION CONNECTIONS

Brandenburg, Jim. *To the Top of the World: Adventures with Arctic Wolves*. 1993. 44p. Walker.

AGES 10–UP   Brandenburg, a wildlife photographer, chronicles his life on remote Ellesmere Island with an Arctic wolf pack.

DeArmond, Dale. *The Seal Oil Lamp: An Adaptation of an Eskimo Folktale.* 1988. 48p. Sierra Club; distributed by Little, Brown.

AGES 8–UP Handsome woodcuts enhance this retelling of a traditional folktale about a blind Eskimo boy who is left to die because he cannot be a hunter or provider.

Ekoomiak, Normee. *Arctic Memories.* 1990. 32p. Holt.

AGES 8–UP Embroidered and appliqued artwork by the author, an Inuit artist, enhances the text, written in both Inuit and English, in this visual and written account of the Inuit culture of years ago.

Fischer, Hank. *Wolf Wars.* 1995. 182p. Falcon.

AGES 10–UP Fischer gives an in-depth account of the wolf restoration program in Yellowstone National Park.

Glubok, Shirley. *The Art of the Eskimo.* 1964. 48p. HarperCollins.

AGES 8–UP An old but useful book that details the various arts of the Inuit, giving examples of masks, carvings, and decorations that adorn their tools and clothing.

Johnson, Sylvia, and Alice Aamodt. *Wolf Pack: Tracking Wolves in the Wild.* 1985. 96p. Lerner.

AGES 10–14 This comprehensive study of the social structure of wolves, their physical characteristics, and their habits includes the role of the wolf in legends handed down through generations.

Lynch, Wayne. *A Is for Arctic: Natural Wonders of a Polar World.* 1996. 144p. Firefly Books.

AGES 8–UP Arranged alphabetically, the full-color photographs invite all readers to visually interact with the land and wildlife of the Arctic.

Martin, Rafe. *The Eagle's Gift.* Illustrated by Tatsuro Kiuchi. 1997. 32p. Putnam.

AGES 8–UP Set in the Alaskan wilderness, this traditional Inuit story is about a boy who brings the gift of joy to his people by singing, dancing, and telling stories.

Northern Tales: Traditional Stories of Eskimo and Indian Peoples. Selected and edited by Howard Norman. 1990. 343p. Pantheon.

AGES 10–UP   These stories reflect the tribal and cultural beliefs of various peoples from the Far North, including the Inuit Eskimos of Alaska.

Patent, Dorothy Hinshaw. *Gray Wolf, Red Wolf.* Photographs by William Munoz. 1990. 64p. Clarion.

AGES 9–12   The life cycle, the social structure and the physical characteristics of wolves are discussed, using numerous color photographs.

San Souci, Robert. *Song of Sedna.* Illustrated by Daniel San Souci. 1981. 32p. Doubleday.

AGES 8–UP   Here, in another picture book for older readers, Sedna, a powerful sea spirit, provides food for her people. This is a powerful, full-color rendition of an old Eskimo legend. Another version is Beverly McDermott's *Sedna: An Eskimo Myth* (Viking, o.p.).

My Brother Sam Is Dead

Four Winds Press   1974   216 pages

JAMES LINCOLN COLLIER AND CHRISTOPHER COLLIER

AGES 10–14

I'd stand at the door and watch them go; and I wondered, if I went for a soldier, which army would I join? The British had the best uniforms and the shiny new guns, but there was something exciting about the Patriots–being underdogs and fighting off the mighty British army.

—Tim Meeker, in My
Brother Sam Is Dead

The American Revolution was a controversial war in the colonies. Many people were still loyal to the English king and saw no reason to form a new nation. Others were tired of the British and their unfair tax laws and felt it was time to break ties to the motherland. As talk of seeking freedom from England spread throughout the colonies, people became agitated and nervous. There were so many different ideas and beliefs about the issues surrounding the war that neighbors were against neighbors, and families against one another. *My Brother Sam Is Dead* is the story of one such family.

Tim Meeker is 64 years old in 1826 when he records his memories of the bloody American Revolution and how it split his family apart. All his life he had looked up to his older brother Sam. At 16 years old, Sam is a student at Yale College. He is known for his intelligence and is admired by everyone in Redding, Pennsylvania, where the Meeker family lives. Life Meeker, the boys' father, is proud of Sam until the day Sam shows up at the family's tavern wearing a uniform and announces, "We've beaten the British in Massachusetts." This announcement comes as a shock to Life Meeker, who didn't know that his son had left school to join the Continental army. Tim, on the other hand, is smitten with Sam's uniform and thinks that Sam looks brave.

When Sam declares to everyone in the tavern that "it's worth dying to be free," Life Meeker is unable to control his anger. "God meant man to obey. He meant children to obey their fathers, he meant men to obey their kings. As a subject of the Lord Our God I don't question His ways. As a subject of His Majesty, George the Third, should you question his ways?" Tim Meeker is confused as he witnesses the bitter fight between his father and brother. Though his father had never been to college, he is sure that his father knows more than Sam does. But, Sam had been to college for one year, and maybe he sees himself as a grownup now.

The exchange of bitter words between father and son continues and Sam storms out of the tavern. When Tim follows him, Sam reveals his real motive in coming home. He had come to get the "Brown Bess," a gun that belongs to his father, to use as his weapon in the war. Sam, who is so sure of his loyalties, tries once again to explain to his father. "Father I am not an Englishman, I am an American, and I am going to fight to keep my country free." Life shouts back, "Go, Sam. Go. Get out of my sight. I can't bear to look at you anymore in that vile costume." At this point, Sam is disowned by his father and gives up his family for the patriot army.

Times continue to be rough for the Meeker family. Tim and his mother worry about Sam, but they don't mention his name in Life's presence. Then, Tim sees Sam one more time when Sam comes to see his girl, Betsy Read, when he is en route to Danbury to buy cattle for the army. This time, Tim tells Sam that his family should be more important to him, and he calls Sam a coward. About this time, Tim begins to realize that his father is not so much a Tory as he is against war. He sees no use for violence, and he doesn't think that any political issue is worth losing innocent lives.

The reality of the war surrounds the citizens of Redding, and the Meeker family can no longer escape the fact that the patriots and the loyalists are officially at war. Though Life Meeker tries to stay out of any discussions about the war with customers at his tavern, it becomes extremely difficult to remain neutral. When Mr. Heron, a Tory, wants Tim to deliver a secret message to Fairfield, Life Meeker says no. He's already lost one son to the war, and he doesn't intend to lose another. Tim lies to his father and tells Mr. Heron that he can make the trip. Along the way, Tim encounters Betsy Read, who convinces him that the message he is delivering is information about Sam. Again, Tim is in a situation where he must question his loyalties.

As the war rages all around, Tim accompanies his father to New York to get supplies for the tavern. They encounter cowboys, and Life Meeker is taken prisoner for selling beef to the British. He eventually dies of cholera on board a prison ship. Tim becomes sickened with the entire idea of the war and the violence that has broken apart his family. He makes his way back to Pennsylvania and prepares to become the man of the family. Then, in 1778, Sam comes to visit one last time. His regiment is camping near Redding, and he slips away to see his mother and brother. He is accused of stealing cattle, and is court-martialed and executed a month later.

Tim Meeker remembers a stern father and a stubborn and brave older brother. He remembers his mother's broken heart at the loss of her husband and her oldest son. And, he wonders "if there might have been another way, beside war, to achieve the same end."

SETTING THE SCENE

Read aloud *Paul Revere's Ride* by Henry Wadsworth Longfellow. Discuss Revere's mission. On April 19, 1775, the first shot is taken, and the American Revolution begins. Discuss why that shot is referred to as the "shot heard around the world."

DISCUSSION

- *My Brother Sam Is Dead* has been challenged by parents across the United States because of "the graphic violence and the use of profanity." How can there be an accurate depiction of war without violence? How does the use of profanity communicate the outrage between the father and son? Try reading the sentences without the profane language. How does it change the tone of the arguments?

- At the beginning of the novel, Sam is trying to explain to his father that the first shot, signaling the beginning of the American Revolution, has been taken. His father asks, "Who do you think fired first?" Sam cannot answer the question and doesn't understand why it matters. Why does it matter to Sam's father to know who fired first? Why doesn't it matter to Sam?

- Define *treason*. Sam states that Massachusetts and Connecticut are ready to fight. Sam's father says that such a discussion is treason. Compare and contrast Sam's views with those of his father. How are their definitions of treason different?

- Sam feels that freedom is worth dying for. What about his upbringing makes him crave freedom? How is Sam's idea of freedom different from his father's?

- Sam's father asks, "Is it worth war to save a few pence in taxes?" Sam replies, "It's not the money, it's the principle." To what principle is Sam referring? How are most wars about principle?

- At what point in the novel does the war become real to Tim?

- How does the war change the Meeker family? Tim says, "The biggest change was within myself." Discuss Tim's passage from boyhood to manhood.

- Tim thinks that Sam is brave, but he doesn't see himself as being brave. How might he define *bravery*? Discuss the moments in the novel when Tim does show bravery.

- Tim questions his loyalties throughout the novel. He says, "Suppose one day we were fighting and I suddenly saw that it was Sam I was aiming my gun at?" Discuss how Tim tries to be loyal to both his father and his brother. How does his father's capture confirm Tim's loyalties? Compare Tim's beliefs about the war at the beginning of the novel to his beliefs at the end.

- Tim is nervous about seeing Sam after their father is captured. He says, "For the first time in my life I knew that Sam was wrong about something. I knew that I understood something better than he did." Discuss what Tim feels that he understands.

- What does Sam's father mean when he says, "In war the dead pay the debts for the living"? Tim feels that before his father died, he had forgiven Sam. Why does Tim blame Sam for his father's death?

ACTIVITIES

- *My Brother Sam Is Dead* has been challenged in schools because some parents feel that the book "contains an inaccurate depiction of the Revolutionary War." Write down all the facts about the Revolutionary War that are revealed in the book. Then, use reference works about the American Revolution to document these facts. Discuss whether the parents' complaints are valid. Why is it important to study historical fiction? How does historical fiction make history more interesting?

- Sam and Tim are taught strict rules regarding sinful behavior. For example, pride and sloth are considered sins in their household. Make a list of other sins that Tim says his father won't tolerate. Then, research the religious beliefs and practices of the Anglican Church. How do Tim's statements about sin reflect the strict teachings of the church in colonial America?

- Although most people in the colonies belonged to the Anglican Church, there were other churches. Find out other denominations that existed in the colonies. Make a chart that contrasts the beliefs of each of these denominations. Which denomination was the biggest threat to the Anglican Church? Find out how religion changed in the colonies after the American Revolution.

- Research the Sugar Act, the Stamp Act, and the Quartering Act. How did these taxation laws contribute to the American Revolution?

- When Sam first joins the rebels, he is in Captain Benedict Arnold's company. Trace Arnold's military career, and find out why he defected and joined the British army.

- Charles Mackubin Lefferts, a self-taught artist, conducted major research on the uniforms worn during the American Revolution. Go to the Web site www.walika.com/ser/uniforms and look at the 26 paintings of soldiers in the American Revolution. Make a stand-alone life-size figure wearing one of the uniforms commonly worn during the American Revolution. Write a historically accurate description of the uniform.

- Many songs were sung during the American Revolution that reflected the views of the loyalists and the British. Using the Internet or books in the library, find the lyrics to the song "The Rebels." This song, written in 1778, is said to illustrate the loyalist point of view. Read the lyrics to the song, and analyze how it communicates the feelings of the loyalists.

- Life Meeker is taken prisoner by the British and dies of cholera on board the prison ship. What other life-threatening diseases did the colonists face during the American Revolution? Find out about these diseases and how they were treated. What conditions of war made the soldiers more susceptible to disease?

- The winter at Valley Forge is considered one of the darkest moments of the American Revolution. Research the problems that George Washington and his troops faced that winter. What other hardships did the Continental army face throughout the war?

- Crispus Attucks is known as the first black man to die for his country. The story of his death is said to be a legend. Find out the details of his death. Why do you think his story is considered a legend?

- George Washington took command of the Continental army on June 15, 1775. Using books in the library or sites on the Internet, research his life and career. Why, do you think, was he chosen to lead the Continental army?

- Patrick Henry delivered his famous "Give me liberty, or give me death" speech on March 23, 1775. Write a story about this speech that might have appeared in a patriot newspaper.

- Draw a map of the colonies, and label all the major battles of the American Revolution. Indicate by color which battles were won by the patriots and which were won by the Tories.

- At the end of the novel, Sam is executed. Write a eulogy that Tim might have written for Sam.

FICTION CONNECTIONS

Avi. *The Fighting Ground*. 1984. 160p. HarperCollins.

AGES 10–12   Thirteen-year-old Jonathan thinks war is glamorous until April 3, 1778, when he is taken prisoner and must wrestle with his own feelings about killing and the horrors of war.

Borden, Louise. *Sleds on Boston Common: A Story from the American Revolution*. Illustrated by Robert Andrew Parker. 2000. Unpaged. Margaret K. McElderry Books.

AGES 9–12   In the winter of 1774, the King of England has closed the Boston Harbor and sent British soldiers to guard the public places.

This doesn't suit young Henry Price, who complains to General Gage that he can't sled on the Boston Common.

Brady, Esther Wood. *Toliver's Secret.* Illustrated by Richard Cuffari. 1993. 176p. Random House.

AGES 9–12   Ten-year-old Ellen Toliver, disguised as a boy, replaces her injured grandfather on a top-secret patriotic mission and gets an important message to General Washington.

Collier, James Lincoln, and Christopher Collier. *War Comes to Willy Freeman.* 1983. 192p. Delacorte.

AGES 10–14   Willy Freeman, a young African American girl, watches as the Redcoats kill her father, and returns home to discover that the British have taken her mother prisoner.

Edwards, Sally. *George Midgett's War.* 1985. 144p. Macmillan.

AGES 9–12   When British raiders steal pigs and murder a deaf woman on Ocracoke Island off the coast of North Carolina, the Revolutionary War takes on a new meaning to the islanders.

Forbes, Esther. *Johnny Tremain.* Illustrated by Lynd Ward. 1962. 256p. Houghton Mifflin.

AGES 9–12   Winner of the 1944 Newbery Medal, this story about 14-year-old Johnny Tremain, a silversmith's apprentice, is set during the American Revolution in Boston and chronicles Tremain's courage and bravery as he becomes personally involved in the war.

Fritz, Jean. *Early Thunder.* Illustrated by Lynd Ward. 1967. 256p. Putnam.

AGES 10–14   As the people in the colonies are choosing sides, a boy in Salem struggles with his decision and shifts his loyalty from King George to the patriots.

Jensen, Dorothea. *The Riddle of Penncroft Farm.* 1989. 192p. Harcourt.

AGES 10–12   Lars solves a current-day mystery and learns about the American Revolution through a ghost from George Washington's day.

Myers, Anna. *Keeping Room.* 1997. 135p. Walker.

AGES 10–UP   During the American Revolution in South Carolina, 13-year-old Joey learns that not all soldiers are good and not all are bad on either side.

O'Dell, Scott. *Sarah Bishop*. 1980. 240p. Houghton Mifflin.

AGES 10–13   Sarah, the daughter of a loyalist, is accused of witchcraft and of setting a fire started by the British, and is befriended by Isaac Morton, a Quaker.

Quackenbush, Robert M. *Daughter of Liberty: A True Story of the American Revolution*. 1999. 64p. Hyperion.

AGES 9–12   Based on a true story that took place during the American Revolution, this novel tells of the heroic and dangerous journey of Wyn Mabie, a woman who volunteers to retrieve important papers for General George Washington in an effort to help him restore his shattered defenses.

Reit, Seymour. *Guns for General Washington: The Impossible Journey*. 1990. 144p. Harcourt Brace.

AGES 9–12   This novel is based on the true story of William and Henry Knox and their mission to transport guns from Fort Ticonderoga to General Washington in the dead of winter.

Rinaldi, Ann. *Cast Two Shadows: The American Revolution in the South*. 1998. 268p. Harcourt Brace.

AGES 12–UP   Fourteen-year-old Caroline Whitaker lives on a plantation in South Carolina and is caught in the middle of the war when her father, a patriot, is imprisoned, her brother, a loyalist, is wounded, and her best friend is hanged by the British.

Rinaldi, Ann. *Finishing Becca: A Story about Peggy Shippen and Benedict Arnold*. 1984. 362p. Gulliver Books.

AGES 12–UP   In Philadelphia in 1778, 14-year-old Becca Synge is the personal maid of wealthy Peggy Shippen and is exposed to deceit and treachery when Shippen influences Benedict Arnold to betray his American forces.

NONFICTION CONNECTIONS

Bober, Natalie S. *Countdown to Independence: A Revolution of Ideas in England and Her American Colonies: 1760–1776*. 2001. 368p. Simon & Schuster.

AGES 12–UP   Bober traces the disagreements between England and her colonies and uses brief biographies of important people, such as Samuel Adams, Thomas Jefferson, and Patrick Henry, to reveal this important era in history.

Carter, Alden. *The American Revolution: War for Independence.* 1992. 64p. Watts.

AGES 10–13   Carter discusses the causes of the American Revolution and gives a comprehensive account of the campaigns and outcome of the war. Other titles in the series are: *The American Revolution: Colonies in Revolt; The American Revolution: Darkest Hours;* and *The American Revolution: At the Forge of Liberty.*

De Pauw, Linda Grant. *Founding Mothers: Women of America in the Revolutionary Era.* 1975. 228p. Houghton Mifflin.

AGES 10–14   The author traces the contribution of women in the colonies during the time of the American Revolution.

Dolan, Edward F. *The American Revolution: How We Fought the War of Independence.* 1995. 110p. Millbrook Press.

AGES 9–12   This comprehensive history of the American Revolution, beginning with the battle of Lexington and ending with the battle of Yorktown, focuses on the roles of famous American patriots and discusses the aftermath of the war and the founding of this nation.

Egger-Bovert, Howard, and Marlene Smith-Baranzini. *Book of the American Revolution.* Illustrated by Bill Sanchez. 1994. 96p. Little, Brown.

AGES 9–12   This chronicle of the events of the American Revolution represents views of both the rebels and the British supporters.

Ferrie, Richard. *The World Turned Upside Down: George Washington and the Battle of Yorktown.* 1999. 160p. Holiday House.

AGES 9–12   This account of the battle of Yorktown, the final battle of the American Revolution, focuses on the leadership of George Washington and his determination to defeat the British forces.

Fradin, Dennis B. *Samuel Adams: The Father of American Independence.* 1998. 182p. Clarion.

AGES 10–UP   The reputation of being responsible for the American Revolution makes Samuel Adams an engaging character, and Fradin dramatically describes his life in this interesting and informative biography.

Fritz, Jean. *And Then What Happened, Paul Revere?* Illustrated by Margot Tomes. c1973, 1996. 45p. Putnam.

AGES 8–12 Most history books recognize Paul Revere for his famous ride, but this biography reveals him as a man, at home making silver spoons, teapots and cups, false teeth, and church bells.

Fritz, Jean. *Why Don't You Get a Horse, Sam Adams?* Illustrated by Trina Schart Hyman. 1974. 47p. Putnam.

AGES 8–12 A humorous biography of Samuel Adams, focusing on his dislike for the King of England and his refusal to conform to what others thought he should be.

Fritz, Jean. *Why Not, Lafayette?* Illustrated by Ronald Himler. 1999. 87p. Putnam.

AGES 9–12 An accurate and lively biography of General Lafayette, the young French general who played an important role in the American Revolution.

Fritz, Jean. *Will You Sign Here, John Hancock?* Illustrated by Trina Schart Hyman. c1976, 1997. 47p. Coward-McCann/Putnam.

AGES 9–12 This biography of the first signer of the Declaration of Independence presents him as a boy, traces his life through his term as governor of Massachusetts, and discusses his numerous contributions to the new nation.

Kent, Deborah. *Lexington and Concord.* 1997. 32p. Children's Press.

AGES 9–12 Part of the Cornerstones of Freedom series, this book discusses the first battles of the American Revolution and the effort it took to unite the 13 British colonies for a common cause.

King, David C. *Benedict Arnold and the American Revolution.* 1999. 80p. Blackbirch.

AGES 10–UP Illustrated with black-and-white prints from the era, this biography of Benedict Arnold focuses on the reasons this gallant soldier became a traitor to his country.

King, David C. *Lexington and Concord.* 1997. 64p. Twenty-First Century Books.

AGES 8–12 Part of the Battlefields across America series, this book focuses on the events that led to the battles at Lexington and Concord.

Koslow, Philip. *John Hancock: A Signature Life.* 1998. 112p. Watts.

AGES 10–UP   This biography presents John Hancock's life, but focuses on his contributions as president of the Second Continental Congress and as governor of Massachusetts.

Marrin, Albert. *War for Independence: The Story of the American Revolution.* 1988. 288p. Atheneum.

AGES 10–14   Marrin gives an accurate account of the American Revolution, its origin, and its outcome.

McGovern, Ann. *The Secret Soldier: The Story of Deborah Sampson.* 1987. 64p. Four Winds Press.

AGES 9–12   This biography tells the fascinating story of Deborah Sampson, who disguised herself as a boy so that she might fight in the American Revolution.

Meltzer, Milton. *American Revolutionaries: A History in Their Own Words– 1750–1800.* 1993. 210p. HarperCollins.

AGES 10–UP   People who lived during the American Revolution are presented through personal letters and journals, making this a valuable resource for understanding the human aspects of this war.

Meltzer, Milton. *Thomas Jefferson: The Revolutionary Aristocrat.* 1991. 256p. Watts.

AGES 10–14   This complicated man is closely examined as one of the major architects of this nation, and his contradiction in character is revealed through a discussion of his views regarding slavery.

Moorem, Kay. *If You Lived at the Time of the American Revolution.* Illustrated by Daniel O'Leary. 1998. 80p. Scholastic.

AGES 9–12   Facts related to daily life during the American Revolution are revealed in a simple but lively question-and-answer format.

Murphy, Jim. *Young Patriot: The American Revolution As Experienced by One Boy.* 1996. 101p. Clarion.

AGES 10–UP   The journals of Joseph Plumb Martin, a soldier in the Revolutionary army, provide material for this stirring account of the suffering and hardships that Martin and all soldiers endured during the entire war.

Osborne, Mary Pope. *George Washington: Leader of a New Nation.* 1991. 96p. Dial.

AGES 9–12   Washington's life is revealed through bits and pieces of authentic diary entries, letters, and speeches.

Peacock, Louise. *Crossing the Delaware: A History in Many Voices.* Illustrated by Walter Krudop and Walter Lyon. 1998. 48p. Atheneum.

AGES 9–12   Excerpts from primary source documents along with letters of a fictional soldier trace the events that led to Washington's crossing of the Delaware River and the battle of Trenton.

Phelan, Mary Kay. *The Story of the Boston Massacre.* Illustrated by Allan Eitzen. 1976. 160p. HarperCollins.

AGES 10–14   This factual account of the Boston Massacre discusses the causes and the results of this important event, and relates the feelings of those who lived in Boston at the time.

Rosenburg, John M. *First in War: George Washington in the American Revolution.* 1998. 224p. Millbrook Press.

AGES 12–UP   Beginning with Washington's appointment as commander-in-chief of the Continental army, this book chronicles his participation in the American Revolution to the end of the war and his famous farewell address.

Zall, P. M. *Becoming American: Young People in the American Revolution.* 1993. 208p. Shoe String/Linnet.

AGES 10–14   The lives and thoughts of young people during the American Revolution are revealed through short excerpts from diaries, journals, and letters.

Zeinert, Karen. *Those Remarkable Women of the American Revolution.* 1996. 96p. Millbrook Press.

AGES 10–13   Through the lives of women like Molly Pitcher, Betsy Ross, and Deborah Sampson, Zeinert reveals the tremendous responsibilities of women during the American Revolution.

BIBLIOGRAPHY

Abel, Richard L. *Speaking Respect, Respecting Speech*. 1998. University of Chicago Press.

Adams, Thelma, ed. *Censorship and First Amendment Rights: A Primer*. 1992. American Booksellers Foundation for Free Expression.

Alderman, Ellen, and Caroline Kennedy. *The Right to Privacy*. 1995. Knopf.

American Library Association Office for Intellectual Freedom and Intellectual Freedom Committee. *Intellectual Freedom Manual*. 5th ed. 1996. American Library Association.

Amey, Lawrence, and others. *Censorship*. 3 vols. 1997. Salem Press.

Anderson, A. J. *Problems in Intellectual Freedom and Censorship*. 1974. Bowker.

Bald, Margaret. *Literature Suppressed on Religious Grounds*. 1998. Facts on File.

Berger, Melvin. *Censorship*. 1982. Franklin Watts.

Brinkley, Ellen Henson. *Caught Off Guard: Teachers Rethinking Censorship and Controversy*. 1999. Allyn and Bacon.

Brown, Jean E. *Preserving Intellectual Freedom: Fighting Censorship in Our Schools*. 1995. National Council of Teachers of English.

Burress, Lee. *Battle of the Books: Literary Censorship in the Public Schools 1950–1985*. 1989. Scarecrow Press.

Burress, Lee, and Edward B. Jenkinson. *Censorship and Education*. 1981. H.W. Wilson.

Burress, Lee, and Edward B. Jenkinson. *The Students' Right to Know*. 1979. National Council of Teachers of English.

Cline, Victor B. *Where Do You Draw the Line? An Exploration into Media Violence, Pornography, and Censorship*. 1974. BYU Press.

Coetzee, J. M. *Giving Offense: Essays on Censorship.* 1996. University of Chicago Press.

Davis, James E. *Dealing with Censorship.* 1979. National Council of Teachers of English.

DelFattore, Joan. *What Johnny Shouldn't Read: Textbook Censorship in America.* 1992. Yale University Press.

Demac, Donna A. *Liberty Denied: The Current Rise of Censorship in America.* 1988. Rutgers University Press.

Foerstel, Herbert N. *Banned in the U.S.A.: A Reference Guide to Book Censorship in Schools and Public Libraries.* 1994. Greenwood Press.

Garry, Patrick. *An American Paradox: Censorship in a Nation of Free Speech.* 1993. Praeger.

Haight, Anne Lyon. *Banned Books, 387 B.C. to 1978 A.D.* 1978. Bowker.

Haiman, Franklyn Saul. *Speech and Law in a Free Society.* 1981. University of Chicago Press.

Heins, Marjorie. *Sex, Sin, and Blasphemy: A Guide to America's Censorship Wars.* 1993. New Press.

Hentoff, Nat. *The First Freedom: The Tumultuous History of Free Speech in America.* 1980. Delacorte.

Hentoff, Nat. *Free Speech for Me but Not for Thee: How the American Left and Right Relentlessly Censor Each Other.* 1993. HarperCollins.

Hentoff, Nat. *Living the Bill of Rights: How to Be an Authentic American.* 1998. HarperCollins.

Hull, Mary. *Censorship in America: A Reference Handbook.* 1999. ABC-Clio.

Hurwitz, Leon. *Historical Dictionary of Censorship in the United States.* 1985. Greenwood Press.

Jensen, Carl. *Censored: The News That Didn't Make the News.* 1996. Four Walls, Eight Windows.

Johnson, Claudia. *Stifled Laughter: One Woman's Fight against Censorship.* 1994. Fulcrum.

Jones, Derek, ed. *Censorship: A World Encyclopedia.* 2001. Fitzroy Dearborn.

Karolides, Nicholas J. *Literature Suppressed on Political Grounds.* 1998. Facts on File.

Karolides, Nicholas J., and others. *Censored Books: Critical Viewpoints.* 1993. Scarecrow Press.

Karolides, Nicholas J., and others. *100 Banned Books: Censorship Histories of World Literature*. 1999. Checkmark.

Kennedy, Sheila Suess, ed. *Free Expression in America: A Documentary History*. 1999. Greenwood Press.

Lehr, Susan, ed. *Battling Dragons: Issues and Controversy in Children's Literature*. 1995. Heinemann.

Levy, Leonard W. *The Establishment Clause: Religion and the First Amendment*. 1994. University of North Carolina Press.

Marsh, Dave. *50 Ways to Fight Censorship*. 1991. Thunder's Newsletter Press.

McWhirter, Darien A. *Freedom of Speech, Press, and Assembly*. 1994. Oryx.

Monks, Merri M., and Donna Reidy Pistolis, eds. *Hit List: Frequently Challenged Books for Young Adults*. 1996. American Library Association.

Noble, William. *Bookbanning in America: Who Bans Books?–and Why?* 1990. Paul S. Eriksson.

Pally, Marcia. *Sex and Sensibility: Reflections on Forbidden Mirrors and the Will to Censor*. 1994. Ecco Press.

Power, Brenda Miller, and others. *Reading Stephen King: Issues of Censorship, Student Choice, and Pop Literature*. 1997. National Council of Teachers of English.

Price, Janet R., and others. *The Rights of Students: The Basic ACLU Guide to a Student's Rights*. 1988. Southern Illinois University Press.

Protecting the Right to Read: A How-to-Do-It Manual for School and Public Libraries. 1995. Neal Schuman.

Reichman, Henry. *Censorship and Selection: Issues and Answers for Schools*. 2001. American Library Association.

Robbins, Louise S. *Censorship and the American Library: The American Library Association's Response to Threats to Intellectual Freedom, 1939–1969*. 1996. Greenwood Press.

Rushdie, Salman, and Michael R. Reder. *Conversations with Salman Rushdie*. 2000. University of Mississippi Press.

Sova, Dawn B. *Literature Suppressed on Sexual Grounds*. 1998. Facts on File.

Sova, Dawn B. *Literature Suppressed on Social Grounds*. 1998. Facts on File.

Steinle, Pamela Hunt. *In Cold Fear: The Catcher in the Rye Censorship Controversies and Postwar America*. 2000. Ohio University Press.

Symons, Ann K., and Charles Harmon. *Protecting the Right to Read*. 1995. Neal Schuman.

West, Mark. *Trust Your Children: Voices against Censorship in Children's Literature*. 1997. Neal Schuman.

Winfield, Betty Houchin. *Bleep! Censoring Rock and Rap Music*. 1999. Greenwood Press.

INDEX

PAT SCALES is director of Library Services at the South Carolina Governor's School for the Arts and Humanities in Greenville, South Carolina. She spent 28 years as a librarian in a middle school and has taught children's literature at Furman University since 1976. She received the ALA/Grolier Award in 1997 and was honored with the AASL/SIRS Intellectual Freedom Award in 1983. Recently, she was named one of the five most influential librarians in the twentieth century in South Carolina. Scales served as chair of the 1992 Newbery Award Committee and the 2001 Laura Ingalls Wilder Committee. She writes teacher's guides for children's and young adult novels for various publishers and is a regular contributor to *Book Links* magazine.